JFK

JFK

HIS LIFE, HIS LEGACY

TIM HILL

Bath · New York · Singapore · Hong Kong · Cologne · Delhi
Melbourne · Amsterdam · Johannesburg · Shenzhen

First published by Parragon in 2013

Parragon
Chartist House, 15–17 Trim Street
Bath, BA1 1HA, U.K.
www.parragon.com

Produced by Atlantic Publishing

ISBN: 978-1-4723-0819-1

Printed in China

Contents

Introduction

John Fitzgerald Kennedy was a high achiever groomed for high office. Born into a competitive hothouse, with politics in the bloodline, Jack Kennedy learned from an early age that winning was all, be it in ball games or elections. The death of his elder brother in wartime service meant ambition and expectation fell on Joseph and Rose Kennedy's second son. There was family wealth to back his rise through the political ranks, yet despite a privileged upbringing, Kennedy faced the twin obstacles of being a social outsider: he came from new money and had Boston-Irish Catholic roots. Both were overcome as the author and war hero climbed the political ladder, elected to the Senate in 1953 after serving six years in the House. Marriage to the glamorous, cultured Jacqueline Bouvier was no hindrance to his hopes of reaching the White House; they were a golden couple who would enjoy the kind of celebrity normally reserved for Hollywood stars.

The young Kennedy was no ideologue, but he had good looks, charisma, charm, and wit, qualities his political opponents underestimated at their peril. He was telegenic in the new televisual age, as Richard Nixon found to his cost in their round of screen sparring prior to the 1960 election. The image—if not the reality—was of robust vitality. Here was a man with the dynamism and vision to galvanize the country after the steady but uninspiring Eisenhower years. At 43, he was the United States's youngest elected president, the first to be born in the twentieth century.

The fruits of JFK's period in office were moderate. Congress impeded many social reforms: civil rights legislation would have to wait for his successor. But the Cuban Missile Crisis revealed his mettle when the stakes were highest, while the quest to put a man on the moon encapsulated the mood abroad that with Kennedy at the helm no barrier was insurmountable. He grew in stature, and by the fall of 1963, was maturing into an outstanding statesman. A new moral dimension informed the decisions he made. The first term had laid the foundations, the second would surely see great strides both on the domestic and international fronts. However, an assassin's bullet robbed the country of that possibility, leaving a crusading idealist a martyr to his reforming cause, a tragic hero.

JFK carried with him the hopes of a generation, inspiring Americans and those beyond his native shores with his ideals, vision, and boundless energy to conquer "new frontiers." His assassination left the world bereft, lamenting the loss of a leader on the cusp of greatness, his promise cruelly unfulfilled. Fifty years after his death, the world remembers John F. Kennedy not so much for his achievements but for what he represented and what might have been.

JFK examines the remarkable Kennedy dynasty, forged in the 1914 union of Joseph Patrick Kennedy and Rose Fitzgerald, a family blessed and cursed in equal measure. It recounts the key moments in the marriage of Camelot's hallowed couple, whose bond survived betrayal and tragedy. And it explores in detail the public and private faces of a towering figure on the twentieth-century political landscape, disentangling myth from reality.

Opposite: JFK and Jackie at Hyannis Port shortly before their marriage.

CHAPTER ONE

Dynastic Roots
1850—1945

John Fitzgerald Kennedy was born on May 29, 1917, the second son to Joseph and Rose Kennedy. The path to the White House was not clearly mapped out for the new arrival, but many elements marking Jack out for high office were in place. Politics was in the blood, on both his father's and his mother's side; drive, ambition, and the will to succeed, at almost any cost, were imbued in him from an early age, and the family was wealthy and well connected. Of course, all of these factors were equally applicable to Jack's elder brother, Joe Jr., but when Joe was killed in action during World War II, the hopes and expectations of the family primarily rested on Jack's shoulders.

Many critical decisions propelled JFK to the White House, with serendipity playing its part. The first of these occurred 69 years before he was born, when 26-year-old Patrick Kennedy, his great-grandfather, joined the teeming exodus from Ireland in the wake of the Potato Famine. Patrick's family grew barley and raised cattle in County Wexford, one of the areas least affected by the blight, but he wanted to broaden his horizons and make his fortune, so he chose to take his chance in the famous "coffin ships" bound for the United States. Many who paid the $12 fare for the grueling six-week journey perished on the way. Patrick was one of the fortunate ones; Bridget Murphy was another. The two struck up a relationship on the crossing, and would marry in September of the following year.

Patrick and Bridget disembarked in Boston and, like many fellow emigrants, settled there. This was primarily an economic decision, for few had the resources to go farther

afield. Living conditions were harsh and those of Irish extraction were subjected to prejudice and hostility from the indigenous population. When employers and landlords posted advertisements in the 1850s, the acronym "NINA" was common: No Irish Need Apply. The establishment was Anglo-Saxon and Protestant. Irish Catholics were looked upon with suspicion and contempt.

Patrick found work as a cooper, while Bridget gave birth to four children in quick succession. The youngest, Patrick Joseph, was born on January 14, 1858. Patrick didn't live to see his son's first birthday, succumbing to cholera two months beforehand. He would be the last of the Kennedy line to die in poverty and obscurity.

Young Patrick, known as P. J., was ambitious and hard-working. In his teenage years, he worked as a stevedore in the shipyards, but in his early twenties he bought a run-down saloon, the first step on the way to a successful business career. P. J.'s talents found a natural home in the political arena. The Irish community formed barroom associations that soon began to dominate local Democratic Party structures. In 1886, P. J. Kennedy began the first of five consecutive terms in the Massachusetts House of Representatives, and in 1892 he was admitted to the state senate. He quickly added political skills to business acumen. A consummate pragmatist, P. J. knew how power and influence were wielded—and he knew what it took to win, something that would become a Kennedy trait.

In 1887, P. J. married Mary Augusta Hickey, the daughter of a prosperous businessman. The couple's first child. Joseph, born on September 6, 1888, was to be the father of the 35th President of the United States.

Opposite: Jack poses with his father Joe while aboard the *Queen Mary* in 1939.

By the turn of the century, P. J. Kennedy was one of the preeminent politicians in Boston. Another was John Francis Fitzgerald, himself a second-generation Irish immigrant. A silky tongued charmer and a larger-than-life character, he became known as "Honey Fitz." He, too, was elected to the state senate in 1892, where he served alongside P. J. The two men had little time for each other. Honey Fitz went on to serve in Congress, and in 1905 he became Boston's first mayor to be born of Irish parents.

The friction between P. J. Kennedy and Honey Fitz was tempered when the two families were joined in marriage. P. J.'s son, Joseph, married Honey Fitz's eldest daughter, Rose, the apple of his eye. Initially, Honey Fitz felt Joseph Kennedy had made the better match, but he changed his mind when he saw the extraordinary talents his son-in-law possessed, and the singlemindedness with which he pursued his goals. Those objectives included becoming a millionaire by the age of 35, which he accomplished with room to spare.

Joe and Rose began married life in a house on Beals Street, Brookline, a well-heeled—and Protestant—area of Boston. The latter fact was particularly significant; Joe fought long and hard to gain the kind of social acceptance that he saw as commensurate with his status within the business community. He found the Brahmins were quick to acknowledge him as a first-rate businessman, but conspired to keep the Kennedys in the second division of Boston's social set. This rankled with Joe, who responded by adding to his wealth even more assiduously. Joe's ultra-competitive spirit was instilled into all his children. Joe Jr., born in 1915, was the first to be imbued with the Kennedy mantra that it wasn't taking part that counted but winning. Jack was the second.

Jack was born in the year the United States entered World War I. His father didn't enlist; instead, he accepted an offer to take over the running of the Fore River Shipyard in Quincy. Shipbuilding was a temporary vehicle for Joe's skills. After leaving Harvard in 1912, he had gone into the banking business. His influence and connections meant he went into the financial sector at a senior level, as state bank examiner. Even so, Joe's ambitions stretched far

Above: Joseph Kennedy and Rose Fitzgerald, whose marriage united two of Boston's most eminent Irish-Catholic families.

beyond that post, and after less than a year in the job he borrowed heavily to take over Columbia Trust, one of the few financial institutions that wasn't hostile to the Irish community.

Joe later diversified into stockbroking, where he displayed astuteness and foresight but he was not above sharp practice. There is also evidence that he crossed the line during the Prohibition era, becoming heavily involved in supplying alcohol illegally until the 13-year ban came to an end in 1933.

Joe's diversification into movies provided ample opportunity for womanizing and, although most liaisons were brief and casual, a passionate affair with screen legend Gloria Swanson nearly destroyed the family. At one point he sought dispensation from the Church to leave Rose and set up home with Swanson, but later the affair fizzled out acrimoniously because of a disastrous project. His eye continued to rove, but the family bond remained fixed and unbreakable. Rose accepted the status quo, as Jackie Kennedy would in similar circumstances a quarter of a century later.

By 1930, when Jack was entering his teenage years, Joe Kennedy had amassed such a fortune that he was able to set up a million-dollar trust fund for each of his children. However, they would not be allowed to rest on their laurels. The work ethic and drive to succeed instilled into all the children ensured there was no room for complacency.

There were now eight in the family. Rosemary was born in 1918, with Kathleen, Eunice, Patricia, Robert, and Jean arriving over the next ten years. Edward was born in 1932. The ethos of the family took no account of gender, and the same tough, competitive streak was instilled into the Kennedy girls. The one family member who struggled in this environment was Rosemary, who was born with a mental impairment and was eventually institutionalized. The family closed ranks, both out of concern for Rosemary's welfare and to avoid the stigma that a public admission would bring. Joe in particular found it hard to come to terms with the situation, equating disability with failure.

Roman Catholicism was central to the Kennedys' lives. Rose was devout, believing religion was the glue that held every facet of an individual's life together. Joe was more pragmatic. He paid lip service to the Church on Sundays, but during the rest of the week did whatever it took to get the job done. When it came to sex and politics, Kennedy males would often find it expedient to relegate morality and piety to a convenient back burner.

Jack Kennedy's early years were in many ways unremarkable—there were typical boyhood scrapes and pranks, and a greater interest in sports than studies. Both academically and in terms of sporting prowess he suffered in comparison to Joe Jr., who was the star of the family. Jack would live for many years in his shadow.

Jack's education began at the Dexter School, a private day school close to the Kennedys' Brookline home. In 1926, Joe moved his family to New York so his children would not face the same barriers he had encountered in Boston. He also felt New York would offer him greater opportunities to expand his business empire, and it was from there that he began commuting regularly to Hollywood.

For Jack, relocating to New York meant changing to Riverdale School, in the suburb where Joe had bought a house overlooking the Hudson River. Three years later the family moved again, to an 11-bedroom mansion in Bronxville. Jack continued his education at Riverdale, but at 13 he was sent to Canterbury School, a Catholic boarding establishment in New Milford, Connecticut. It was the first time he had been away from home and no doubt was yet another stage in the character-building program that his father so carefully orchestrated.

Jack was an avid reader, particularly during the long periods of confinement he had to endure through a succession of illnesses. Unfortunately, the reading matter he absorbed failed to translate into academic distinction or even half-decent spelling. His strengths were his personal qualities: charm, wit, and a well-developed sense of humor.

At Choate, a college preparatory school in Wallingford, Connecticut, the pattern continued; Joe Jr. remained two years in front of him chronologically and well ahead in academic and sporting prowess. Jack graduated from Choate in 1935, when he was 18 years old. There were times when it seemed he wouldn't survive in a seat of learning full of highfliers. He did knuckle down in his final year, yet it only pushed him up to a mediocre 64th in a year group of 112. Nevertheless, it was the personable young man who had scraped through who was voted by classmates as the most likely to succeed.

Perhaps in an effort to assert his independence, Jack opted to go to Princeton; Joe Jr. had followed in his father's footsteps and was already at Harvard. In the summer of 1935, Jack traveled to England to study under socialist economist Harold Laski at the London School of Economics. Although the principles Laski espoused were anathema to a tycoon, an understanding of a left-wing economic perspective was important to provide a counterbalance to the wealth and privilege of his upbringing. In the event, illness forced Jack to return home early, and by the spring of 1936, he had decided that he did not want to take up a place at Princeton a year behind his friends from Choate. He would go to Harvard after all.

In his first two years at Harvard, Jack again tried to match the sporting achievements of his older brother, but it was a case of guts and determination rather than athletic ability. A severe back injury sustained during a football match ended his hopes in that arena and led to further back problems throughout his life. In true Kennedy style, however, he tried out for the swim team instead. He also began to establish a reputation as a ladies' man.

Jack's political awakening now began to manifest itself. He read Churchill's words on the growing Nazi threat; Republicans and Fascists were fighting for the soul of Spain, and at home Roosevelt was wrestling with the Depression. There was much to occupy the thoughts of a political science undergraduate. The ideas and principles that shaped JFK's political beliefs became further crystallized with a trip to Europe in summer 1937. In December that year, the family's political fortunes improved when Joe was appointed U.S. ambassador to Britain. Joe felt the post was a long-overdue reward befitting the support given to Roosevelt over two successful presidential campaigns.

Joe took up the post in April 1938. The following spring, with Europe on the brink of war, Jack asked the Harvard authorities for special leave to go on a fact-finding tour of Europe on behalf of his father. He spent several months traveling in Europe and the Middle East and used the information gathered as the subject for his final-year thesis. Eventually edited and published under the title *Why England Slept*, the book became an instant best seller. Inevitably, Joe had a hand; he bought a huge number of copies, ensuring widespread coverage for the work and an enhanced profile for its author. And at last Jack had found a sphere in which he eclipsed Joe Jr.—but war was to bring a family tragedy and leave Jack as the sole incumbent of the starring role.

Jack left Harvard with an bachelor's degree in political science in June 1940, when Allied forces in Europe were experiencing some of their darkest moments. He briefly attended Stanford University's business school that fall, just as his father was returning from his ambassadorial duties in England. Father and son were as one in their view that the United States should maintain an isolationist policy. For Joe, this meant an irrevocable rift with Roosevelt; he had decided to support FDR's bid for a third term in the White House, but when the latter was successfully returned, Kennedy resigned.

The United States' entry into the war was still a year away, but both Jack and Joe Jr. enlisted. Joe Jr. joined the U.S. Naval Reserve and began flight training. Jack should have failed a services medical, but Joe pulled strings and his second son was assigned to Naval Intelligence in Washington. Joe was fiercely protective of his sons and had not wanted them to risk their lives in a fight that was nothing to do with the United States, but now backed them wholeheartedly: war offered the perfect opportunity to put the Kennedy virtues into practice. Jack was working at Naval Intelligence when Pearl Harbor was attacked, precipitating the country's entry into the war.

In the spring of 1940, Jack's back problem worsened and surgery was recommended but ultimately deferred. He reported to Northwestern University for officer training where he signed up for PT boat duty. These plywood-hulled boats were fast and maneuverable but notoriously unreliable and vulnerable. PT duty was highly dangerous, which made it a glamorous option for Jack, who longed to see active combat. There was another reason for his impatience; Joe Jr. had just earned his wings and joined the Naval Reserve, an elite group; PT duty was a way of redressing the competitive balance between the brothers. Jack suffered a brief setback when he was made an instructor after completing his training at Melville, Rhode Island, but in March 1943 he was on his way to the Solomon Islands in the South Pacific. He was given command of PT-109, and in mid-July was sent to the front line. But on August 2, an incident occurred that became shrouded in mystery, one in which Jack was by turns hero and villain. PT-109 was on patrol in Blackett Strait when it was rammed by a Japanese destroyer. The boat exploded and two of the crew were killed; others were badly injured, including Patrick McMahon, who suffered terrible burns. A small,

Above: Joe and Rose pose with their children, with the exception of Joe Jr., on the beach at Hyannis Port.

highly maneuverable PT boat should never have allowed itself to be hit by such a large vessel, and Kennedy's leadership was later called into question. However, over the next five days he redeemed himself with acts of bravery that ensured the survival of the rest of his crew. The exhausted men made it to three islands, while Jack personally towed McMahon for miles. He also swam out alone in dangerous waters seeking an Allied vessel. Rescue finally came when they were spotted by friendly local people, who reported their position to American forces. Kennedy was recommended for the Silver Star, but eventually received the more modest Navy and Marine Corps Medal; the authorities chose to focus on the part he played in his crew's survival rather than any errors of judgment that precipitated the predicament. Jack and his father made great political capital out of the incident in later years.

Kennedy returned to the United States at the end of 1943 and spent six months with an easy posting in Florida. He was finally hospitalized for back surgery in June 1944, and while recuperating he learned of Joe Jr.'s death. Perhaps frustrated by Jack's celebrated exploits while he had been kicking his heels, Joe Jr. had volunteered for a highly dangerous bombing mission. His aircraft was loaded with 20,000 pounds of explosives and Joe set out for France to knock out V2 launching ramps. He was to bail out after setting the fuses, but the explosives detonated prematurely. He was 29 years old.

The loss of the family's golden boy was a shattering blow and hit Joe particularly hard. By the time Jack was discharged from the military on health grounds in early 1945, the hopes and dreams harbored for Joe's firstborn had transferred to his second. Jack became only too aware of the level of expectation that now rested on his shoulders.

First tragedy

Left: Rose Kennedy nurses Rosemary on her lap, with Joe Jr. (left) and John. Rosemary became the family's first tragic figure. Her intellectual development was impaired, and she became a fringe member of the family circle. Joe in particular failed to come to terms with having a child unable to compete and achieve.

Below: Brookline, Massachusetts, 1919. Joe Jr. and Jack pose with their father on the running board of the family car. Having made a lot of money managing a shipyard during the war, Joe added to his fortune with stock market dealings that sometimes verged on sharp practice. He also diversified into motion pictures and the liquor business with equal success.

Opposite: Joseph and Rose Kennedy's marriage survived many acts of infidelity. The most infamous of Joe's affairs involved the silent screen star Gloria Swanson. When he invited Swanson to accompany him and Rose on a trip to Europe, the actress was left wondering whether his wife was "a fool or a saint."

Rivalry and friendship

Above: Jack (pulling cart) with siblings (left to right) Kathleen, Rosemary, Eunice, and Joe Jr. Along with Rosemary, Jack gave his parents most cause for concern because he was often sick. Eunice was precocious and intelligent, while Kathleen was the most vivacious of the girls. Due to Rosemary's disability, "Kick" as Kathleen was known, would assume seniority among the Kennedy girls.

Right: Ten-year-old Jack sporting the football colors of Dexter School, Brookline. Athletic pursuits and a tight family bond were a feature of the Kennedys' upbringing, but Jack's performances were notable more for endeavor than skill. As a young scholar Jack lacked application and was a notoriously bad speller. He was also frequently in trouble for typical boyhood scrapes and misdemeanors. However, during his long periods of confinement through illness, he was a voracious reader and books would be a lifelong passion.

Opposite: Jack and Joe Jr.'s relationship was one of fierce rivalry as well as fraternal friendship. During their formative years, Jack lived in the shadow of his older brother, both academically and in the field of sporting endeavor.

Different childhoods

Above: August 12, 1934. The Bouvier family attends a horse show on Long Island. Jackie's parents first separated in 1936, when Jackie was seven. After the marriage ended, she and her younger sister, Lee, went to live with their mother, with whom Jackie had a turbulent relationship. Jackie adored her father, despite the fact that he was vain, feckless, and unfaithful. She admired the fact that he was a fun-loving reveler, and in her adult relationships she was drawn to men whose characters had a dangerous edge. Jack Kennedy fitted the bill in this respect, and in some ways reminded her of her father.

Opposite above: The Kennedys in 1934: (left to right) Edward, Jean, Robert, Patricia, Eunice, Kathleen, Rosemary, Jack, Rose, and Joe Sr. The Kennedy family was completed with the birth of a ninth child, Edward, in 1932. The children were ultra-competitive, but were quick to close ranks against any perceived external threat. All its members vied for the attention and approval of Joe Kennedy, whom Rose dubbed the "architect of our lives."

Opposite below: Jack (standing third left) joined the Harvard Swim Team after a back injury ended his footballing days. Sports and socializing occupied a lot of Jack's time during his college years. However, his senior thesis on the the appeasement policy of the Chamberlain government in Britain during the late 1930s earned him great distinction.

The young author

Left: In the summer of 1937, the end of his freshman year at Harvard, Jack traveled to Europe with Lem Billings, a fellow student who would become a lifelong friend. In letters home Jack made some broad-brush observations about the political situation in Spain, Italy, the Soviet Union, and England, but the trip was mainly for hedonistic pursuits.

Opposite above: As usual, the sporting theme shows through in this family picture, with Teddy (kneeling) and Eunice (right) holding footballs. Teddy, the baby of the family, was a prankster and joker and much indulged by his siblings and parents. Missing are Joe Jr., Rosemary, and Kathleen. Rosemary's absences were often explained away as "shyness." Rosemary adored her father, despite his coolness toward her. Joe was harsh about his eldest daughter's lack of intellectual capabilities, and was also critical of her tendency to put on weight. In 1941 he agreed to let doctors perform a lobotomy on Rosemary, an experimental and highly dangerous operation. It made her condition worse and she became institutionalized thereafter.

Opposite below: A family photography taken in 1938, the year Joe Kennedy was appointed U.S. ambassador to Great Britain.

Bravado on the slopes

Left: Jack vacationing in Cannes with Patricia (left) and Eunice. Eunice was intelligent and devoutly religious. Pat was widely regarded as the most beautiful of the Kennedy girls.

Below: Patricia, Eunice, Robert, and Joe Jr. taking skiing lessons during a vacation in San Moritz at the end of 1938. Joe, Robert, and Teddy all sustained limb injuries in quick succession as their natural bravado came to the fore. The Kennedys were by now a celebrated family on both sides of the Atlantic.

Bound for Britain

Above: March 1938. Rose Kennedy and five of the children on board the SS *Washington*, bound for England to join Joe, the recently appointed ambassador. The two eldest sons remained at Harvard. Jack was in his sophomore year, while Joe Jr. was set to graduate that summer. Rose was acutely aware of the importance of this diplomatic posting, both politically and socially. She had long harbored thoughts that Roosevelt might offer the ambassadorship to Joe, and wrote to the President saying that the family were "honored, delighted, and thrilled" at his decision. Joe and Rose took up residence at 9 Prince's Gate, the palatial embassy building donated to the United States by philanthropist John Pierpont Morgan. They were quickly absorbed into fashionable society, with Rose showing far greater sensitivity to protocol than her plain-speaking husband. Joe was eager to make his mark by helping shape U.S. foreign policy; Rose organized the large embassy retinue and took a close interest in introducing her elder daughters into society.

High society

Above: London, April 1938. Kathleen and Bobby riding out on Rotten Row in London shortly after their father's appointment as ambassador to Britain. Kathleen entranced a string of the country's most eligible bachelors. She would marry the man considered the most eligible of them all, Billy Hartington, son of the Duke of Devonshire. Rose Kennedy refused to give her blessing to a match between her daughter and a Protestant suitor, causing a rift within the family.

Opposite above: The ambassador returned to the United States briefly in June 1938, determined to further his twin ambitions: preventing his country from being drawn into a European conflict, while keeping one eye firmly fixed on the presidential election of 1940. He returned to Europe with Jack and Joe Jr. aboard the SS *Normandie* at the end of June. Joe Sr. became an increasingly marginalized political figure during his tenure as ambassador to Britain—President Roosevelt began to distance himself, and there were soon calls for Kennedy's resignation over his perceived compliant attitude over Nazism. He was also accused of anti-Semitism.

Opposite below: Jacqueline Bouvier, at the age of ten, at the Tuxedo Horse Show with her mother (right) and a family friend. Janet and her two daughters finally moved out of the family home at East Hampton in the summer of 1938 and the Bouviers were divorced in June 1940. The acrimonious split deeply affected Jackie, who developed the capacity to block out pain, something that would serve her well in later life.

Kennedys received by new Pope

Above: The Kennedy family are received at the Vatican. Rose's devout faith made this one of the defining moments in her life. They had met the new Pope, Pius XII, when, as Cardinal Pacelli, he visited the United States in November 1936. He had taken tea at the family's Bronxville home, and thereafter Rose had not allowed anyone to sit on the chair he had occupied. The girls, under Rose's influence, were more devout. The boys took their lead from Joe, who was of the view that a weekly dose of piety was quite enough. The rest of the week was for the masculine pursuits of business and pleasure.

Right: Jack's travels in the spring and summer of 1939 included a visit to Egypt. At this point he had the best of both worlds, rubbing shoulders with royalty and high-ranking diplomats, yet with ample opportunity to escape from the spotlight. In one celebrated escapade in the south of France, he overturned his car on the way to a party and was lucky to escape serious injury. The role of number two son undoubtedly had its advantages.

Opposite: At a Fourth of July Garden Party, held at London's American Embassy, 1939. Jack dissented from the widespread view that Europe would erupt into war before the year was over.

"War would drain us"

Opposite: Joe and Rose Kennedy, pictured at their Palm Beach home in 1940. Relations between Kennedy and President Roosevelt reached rock bottom late in the year, culminating in the former resigning as ambassador to Britain. With the death of Neville Chamberlain and the elevation of Winston Churchill to Britain's premiership, Kennedy's political isolation was complete. Free of the strictures of diplomatic office, he continued to voice his extreme opinions, commenting in one interview that "war would drain us" and "democracy is finished in England." His virulent antiwar stance had domestic roots too: he wanted to protect his sons from a battle he felt was nothing to do with the United States.

Above: Palm Beach, February 11, 1940. Joe and Rose Kennedy celebrate Rose's father's 77th birthday. With Joe's political fortunes waning, the mantle passed to his eldest son. Joe Jr. was a delegate at the 1940 Democratic Convention, although he needed his grandfather Honey Fitz to pull some strings in order to secure his seat. Influenced by his father, Joe Jr. also adopted firm isolationist views.

Left: Eunice, Bobby, and Jean, pictured at Palm Beach in January 1941. Jean, born February 20, 1928, was the youngest of the five Kennedy daughters.

Into battle

Opposite: Lieutenant John F. Kennedy was made captain of PT-109 in March 1943. Both Jack and Joe Jr. signed up for military service before the United States entered the war. Jack's health problems may well have precluded him from active duty, but his father used his influence to ensure he passed the medical examination. Joe had initially wanted to keep his sons out of the war, but he came to regard the conflict as a vehicle for them to show their natural competitiveness and leadership skills.

Right: Jack, pictured with some of his PT crew members. Paul "Red" Fay (right) became a close friend and served as Under Secretary of the Navy during Kennedy's presidency.

Above: A family gathering at Palm Beach. The war years saw the family's three most charismatic members assert their independence. Joe Jr. and Jack were both on active duty. Kathleen joined the Red Cross as a means of returning to England and renewing her relationship with Billy Hartington. The two would marry on May 6, 1944, with only Joe Jr. representing the Kennedy family. Hartington was killed in action on September 8.

The war hero

Above: June 13, 1944. Lieutenant Kennedy is congratulated by Capt. F. L. Conklin after receiving the Navy and Marine Corps Medal. In the early hours of August 2, 1943, PT-109 was rammed by the Japanese destroyer *Amagiri* in Blackett Strait in the Solomon Islands. Two crewmen were killed, while others were badly injured. Despite the fact that he had been in command when the highly maneuverable PT boat was rammed, Kennedy was recommended by his commanding officer for the more prestigious Silver Star for his "extremely heroic conduct." After investigating the role Kennedy played in the survival phase of the incident, the naval authorities decided that the lesser award was more appropriate, for the valor and leadership Kennedy had shown during the five-day ordeal before the crew were rescued.

Opposite: Kennedy cuts a dashing figure during his naval service days. He returned from his nine-month tour of duty in the South Pacific a war hero, something he and his family would make much of during his political career.

CHAPTER TWO

Formidable Candidate and Flawed Husband 1945–1959

Jack had been considering several peacetime career options, but the pressure for him to make a name for himself in politics was overwhelming. Of course, the Kennedy machine would not let it be known that Jack had chosen this route by default. That would have suggested a lack of conviction, passion, and vision. And in the early days he was certainly no consummate performer on the political stage; he was not a natural orator, but his charm and magnetism were there for all to see.

Before he engaged in his first political battle, Jack worked as a journalist—his father called in favors to secure him a job as a special correspondent for Hearst newspapers. He covered the Potsdam Conference, the first meetings of the United Nations, and the general election in Britain. During the latter it is said he predicted that Churchill would be comfortably returned when in fact the result was a Labour Party landslide. The pieces he wrote during this brief tenure were of no great quality, nor did they offer any particular insight. However, they placed him alongside the most important movers and shakers in world politics and helped to raise his own profile.

There was a setback in August 1945, when Jack became violently ill during his visit to London. Details of his medical condition were rarely forthcoming, though it seems likely that he had fallen victim to Addison's disease. This is a failure of the adrenal glands, the symptoms including weight loss and a yellowish skin pigmentation. He returned home to concentrate on mounting the first rung of the political ladder. Massachusetts was targeted as the launchpad for Jack's new career; the Congressional seat for the 11th District was to be the first battleground. This was P. J. Kennedy's and Honey Fitz's old stamping ground, and where his father had been born. Even so, allegations of carpetbagging were widespread.

James Curley was the target seat's incumbent, but he vacated it in the fall of 1945 after winning Boston's mayoral election for the fourth time. Jack established residency in the city early in 1946, renting a room at the Bellevue Hotel. Because the seat Jack was fighting was Democratic to the core, it was the primary that was the key vote. His early efforts out on the stump were not overly impressive, but he worked hard on his speeches, practicing his delivery exhaustively, and there was considerable improvement. Even so, the campaign was based more on personality than on issues. Jack even made a virtue out of being resolutely non-doctrinaire—if elected, he said he would tackle each issue on its merits. He was for jobs and against extremism of both the left and right. One cause that was close to his heart was housing, particularly for war veterans. Inevitably, the recent conflict played an important part in the campaign. He gave a talk to Gold Star mothers, those who had lost a son in the fighting, and pointed out that his own mother was one of their number. And predictably, the heroic aspects of events involving PT-109 were highlighted. The overriding impression was of a slick marketing exercise with Kennedy money liberally dispensed. Some of this was

Opposite: Jack's good looks didn't impress all the Democrat grandees, but they underestimated the power of his personal appeal.

Above: The congressman, pictured with sisters Eunice (left) and Jean.

handed out to individuals to cover expenses incurred or for any service rendered. Political opponents complained bitterly that it was tantamount to greasing palms.

With the whole Kennedy family working feverishly in the background, the campaign was well-organized, polished—and successful. Jack beat off the challenge of the nine other Democratic candidates in the June primary, receiving twice as many votes as his nearest rival. And in November 1946, victory over the Republican candidate was the formality everyone anticipated. Jack Kennedy, 29, had taken his first step to the White House.

Jack took his seat in the 80th Congress in January 1947, already tipped by many as a rising star. The fact that there was a Republican majority in both Houses made it even easier for an outstanding young Democratic congressman to catch the eye. Or it would have, had Kennedy shown any great talent or made his mark on the chamber. But having done what Kennedys were good at—winning—the newly elected congressman exhibited little desire or interest in the affairs of state. He joined several committees, including the Education and Labor Committee, but he embraced no great cause, revealed no lively enthusiasm for the daily business of Congress. His attendance record was woeful, and although his continuing poor health was at least partly responsible, this didn't seem to keep him from his two other main interests: sports and socializing.

His peers, both political allies and foes, quickly got his measure. Many saw him as a lightweight, a lot of froth and little substance. Unsurprisingly, Joe Kennedy took a different view. He had staked a lot on his second son; the investment was emotional as well as financial, and Joe already harbored thoughts of a bid for the White House in 1960. With the ultimate prize as the long-term goal, Kennedy Sr. continued to keep close tabs on his son's professional and personal life, and Jack continued to defer to his father's judgment on any number of issues. Many of Jack's contemporaries might have found Joe's lofty ambitions for his son laughable. But in an era in which the media was burgeoning, JFK would be the first person to show that being photogenic and telegenic was a far more powerful political weapon than any amount of worthy, painstaking committee work on some minor bill.

In 1947, Jack embarked on a fact-finding tour of Europe but became ill in Ireland, where he had stopped off to visit his sister Kathleen. His condition worsened when he reached London, and hospital tests confirmed Addison's disease. He returned home immediately and last rites were administered. Later, cortisone treatment would keep the condition in check but Jack's political opponents would confront him with the truth on more than one occasion. Weakness was not part of the Kennedy vocabulary and Jack would continue to assert that his recurring bouts of illness were due to malaria contracted in the South Pacific.

In May 1948, the Kennedys were rocked by another tragedy. Kathleen, known as "Kick," was killed in a plane crash along with her lover, Peter Milton, Lord Fitzwilliam. Jack was distraught; "Kick" was his favorite sister and her death made him consider his own mortality. It also made him even more anxious to live each day to the full, and that meant an even greater turnover of women in his life. His interest in the daily grind on Capitol Hill waned still further.

In 1951, Jack traveled to Israel and the Far East, meeting such high-profile figures as Ben Gurion and Nehru. He visited Vietnam and was apprised of the conflict between the French colonial power and the Communist Vietminh. The defeat of the French at Dien Bien Phu was still three years away, after which the United States would become increasingly embroiled in Indochina. A decade after his fact-finding visit Jack would continue to wrestle with the same problems, only as president, not congressman.

Although Jack could now speak with some authority on foreign affairs, the Senate seat targeted for the 1952 election would be no pushover. The incumbent was Henry Cabot Lodge Jr., grandson of one of Honey Fitz's old sparring partners. He had been a senator for the best part of 20 years, and seen off many a Democratic challenge. And before he could take on the confident Cabot Lodge, it was necessary to secure the Democratic nomination. That cause was helped when Governor Paul Dever decided to run for another term in office rather than try for the Senate. Joe Kennedy may well have had a hand in helping Dever reach his decision, one that left the way clear for Jack.

The Kennedy machine swung into action. All the family contributed, with 26-year-old Bobby cutting his political teeth as campaign manager. He carried off the role with ruthless efficiency, although it was Joe pulling the important strings offstage. The usual tactics were employed, focusing on Jack's youth, vitality, and personality. His war exploits were revisited ad nauseam. Here was a man of principle and ideals, although he demurred from being too specific about any of them.

In a ceaseless round of tea parties and glad-handing, voters were treated to a combination of Hollywood-style glamour and homespun homilies. There were two television debates in which Jack held his own against Lodge. With no great policy differences between the two, it came down to image and presentation. That played to the Kennedy strengths and Jack duly won by 70,000 votes. The newly elected senator took his seat in January 1953.

Jack was widely acknowledged as one of the most eligible bachelors in the country, something he played upon when pressing the flesh with the seemingly endless stream of young single women during the campaign tea parties. But by June 1951, he had already met his future bride, Jacqueline Bouvier, at a dinner party. She was 23, twelve years his junior, and had recently graduated from George Washington University. She was working as a photographer at the *Washington Times-Herald*. The Bouviers had been extremely wealthy and had the class and bearing that the Kennedy family aspired to achieve. By the early 1950s, their fortune had been largely dissipated but Jackie's cultured ways and breeding remained. She was also very beautiful.

Jackie had had a troubled childhood. Her mother, Janet, and father, Jack, had a stormy marriage—"Black Jack" was a feckless philanderer and Janet was naturally volatile, so the sparks regularly flew. Jackie and her younger sister, Lee, were not shielded from these domestic battles, and they had a profound effect. Jackie learned a cool detachment during this formative period; it wasn't her natural way to be unemotional and aloof but she decided keeping the world at arm's length was the key to being more secure, less vulnerable. She was seven when her parents separated

Above: The Kennedys were regarded as a golden couple when they married at St. Mary's Church, Newport, on September 12, 1953.

in 1936. Both children went to live with their mother but Jackie disliked Janet, who had regularly turned her guns on her eldest child to sublimate her anger with her husband. Jack, by contrast, was an indulgent father and for all his faults Jackie adored him.

Jackie's difficult relationship with her mother persisted long after the divorce from Jack and remarriage to investment banker Hugh Auchinloss. Janet often undermined her eldest daughter, who reminded her of her reviled ex-husband. Jackie became introspective and immersed in art, literature, and history. In particular she had a voracious appetite for French culture, no doubt feeling a natural affinity to her father's roots. Janet felt being intelligent and opinionated would be a handicap in landing a suitable husband; her constant sniping took its toll, and Jackie suffered from low self-esteem. She deliberately adopted a kind of look, mannerisms, and persona that her mother had convinced her men found most attractive.

One thing the two women did have in common was an awareness of the need to make a good match. Jackie eventually became engaged to a stockbroker, a safe if unremarkable choice. But when the most eligible bachelor in the land began paying attention to her, the engagement was quickly called off. Jack's good looks, intelligence, charm, wealth, and position naturally drew her to him, while to know such a desirable man was interested in her boosted Jackie's flagging self-confidence. For Jack's part, he thought her classy and erudite, as well as beautiful. That she was well read and had a passion for the arts and history were added attractions, not the handicap Janet had predicted.

Jack may have found Jackie interesting and attractive, but marriage was a huge step for a serial womanizer. However, Joe Kennedy thought a wife would be perfect for Jack's career, and Jack proposed in May 1953. Jackie was well aware of the number of women who aspired to become Mrs. John F. Kennedy. Her initial response was to decamp with a girlfriend to London, where she combined sightseeing with work for the *Times-Herald*. Even so, her answer to Jack's proposal was not in doubt for long. He promptly took off for a vacation in Europe. It was not to be a last fling; fidelity was not going to be his strong suit.

They were married at Newport, Rhode Island, on September 12, 1953. Naturally, it was a lavish affair, with Bobby doing the honors as best man. The newlyweds honeymooned in Acapulco and looked every inch a golden couple, but the cracks began to show almost immediately. Jackie had a starry-eyed vision of becoming actively involved in her husband's work, a natural outlet for her intellect and curiosity. However, she quickly reached the conclusion that politics was a tedious business. Even more worrying, her new husband wanted to have his marital cake and continue to dine as a bachelor. The humiliation she had sometimes suffered at her mother's hands returned in a different guise, for Jack showed little discretion in his amorous pursuits. The same defense mechanism she had employed as a child during her own parents' bitter struggles again came into play. She became detached and aloof.

In mid-1955, the Kennedys moved into a $125,000 house in McClean, Virginia. With Jack absent for long periods, Jackie devoted her talent and energy to a grand refurbishment plan. Despite the Kennedy wealth, Jack was notoriously poor at handling money. He rarely carried cash, often borrowing from friends and aides when the need arose. Jackie's extravagant outlay on their new home, far from pleasing the senator, merely irked him.

The house move came as Jack was recovering from a major back operation. The highly risky double-fusion procedure had been carried out the previous October, but an infection set in and he lapsed into a coma. Last rites were again administered. The subsequent convalescence was slow and painful but was also notable on both personal and professional fronts; with Jackie in attendance and philandering off the agenda, the marriage enjoyed a period of harmony. Jack formulated ideas for a book, *Profiles In Courage*, which documented figures in the US's political history who had shown unswerving adherence to their principles in the face of adversity. He used Jackie as a sounding board and she also carried out research.

Jack's incapacity also meant that he conveniently missed a key vote on one of the most controversial political figures of the day. Senator Joe McCarthy's notorious "witch hunts" against public figures who may have had Communist sympathies had become so extreme that the Senate decided to act. He faced a censure motion on December 2, 1954. Jack's stance on Communism was almost as fervent as McCarthy's, and he was a family friend. On the other hand, Jack had the liberal wing of the Democratic Party to consider. He was still bedbound when the vote was taken and used this as a convenient excuse for failing to register his vote. He was the only member of his party who failed to declare, and his opponents were quick to conclude that he avoided the issue. He finally went on record saying that he would have voted for censure, but only some 18 months later.

Profiles In Courage was published in 1956. It was an instant best seller and was awarded a Pulitzer Prize the following year. As well as lauding the achievements of an array of political heavyweights, including John Quincy Adams and Robert Taft, the book raised Jack's own profile several notches. The reader no doubt saw the author as a man of integrity and principle, someone who thought deeply about both his political heritage and the issues of the day. Jack basked in the glory and kudos accorded him by its success, although the integrity of the authorship was questioned. A key figure in both the research and drafting of the work was Ted Sorensen, who had joined Jack's staff early in 1953 when he was 24 years old. An attorney by profession, Sorensen had impressed Kennedy with his intelligence and painstaking attention to detail. He was also a wonderful speechwriter, and the combination of his prose style and Jack's delivery would prove to be a formidable weapon up to the presidential campaign and beyond. Sorensen's other main attribute was a fierce loyalty and he himself insisted that his boss was the sole author of *Profiles In Courage*.

The presidential election was held in 1956; Eisenhower was seeking another term and Jack was in contention as running mate to Adlai Stevenson. Stevenson had been beaten by Eisenhower four years earlier and had major

Above: Bobby, the younger brother by eight years, married Ethel Skakel (second left) in 1950. Ethel had much of the Kennedy spirit, whereas many of the family traits and pastimes left Jackie cold.

reservations as to whether including Kennedy on the ticket would help his cause this time. Jack said he was not seeking the vice-presidency, but let it be known that he would accept the nomination should it be offered. Stevenson was still unsure; despite his obvious qualities and appeal, Kennedy was seen by many as young, inexperienced, and lacking the intellect required for high office. And regardless of the sentiments expressed in the Bailey Memorandum, a document penned by Sorensen to allay fears that a Catholic candidate would be a net vote loser, many influential figures in the Democratic Party thought the country was not yet ready for a Catholic on a presidential ticket.

In a move that stunned delegates, Stevenson threw the choice of running mate over to the floor instead of naming his own man. In the ensuing vote Jack lost out narrowly to Estes Kefauver, the man whom Stevenson had beaten for the presidential nomination. Jack was gracious in defeat, but behind the smiles of support he was hugely disappointed. The despondency wasn't to last long, as the Democrats crashed to an even heavier defeat than in 1952. Jack remained untainted by the Republican landslide and in hindsight came to view his failure to secure the vice-presidential nomination as a stroke of fortune; he could set his sights on the 1960 election with a clean bill of health.

Jack should have been buoyed by the imminent birth of his first child. Jackie was pregnant during the Democratic convention, but after losing out to Kefauver Jack sought solace and rest in a Mediterranean vacation. Jackie had already suffered a miscarriage during their first year of marriage, and her doctor advised her against an overseas trip. Jack saw no reason to amend his plans, so Jackie was sent to stay with her mother. They were still separated by the Atlantic Ocean when Jackie began to hemorrhage and was rushed into hospital. An emergency Cesarean was performed but the child, a baby girl, was stillborn. Bobby hurried to his sister-in-law's bedside and two days later presided over the funeral. When Jack was finally reached, he took the news calmly and saw no reason to return home. The fact that Jackie herself had been seriously ill in addition to the psychological impact of losing a second child seemed to elude him. It was a callous act and a watershed in their relationship. Ultimately, however, Jackie chose the status quo, with all the hurt and difficulties that went with it. Jackie, at least in part, blamed herself for her husband's dalliances. In short, the marriage wasn't perfect, it wasn't what she wanted or expected, but she decided to settle for it.

Meanwhile, Jack had articulated his intention to run for president, which meant four long years of exhaustive campaigning. Jackie had wanted to use her talents to support his bid, but in the event she remained a peripheral figure. There were two reasons: Jack's inner circle of advisers suggested that Jackie might be perceived as lacking the common touch; on a more practical note, early in 1957 she became pregnant again. Jack now didn't have to worry about a potential liability to the cause, while Jackie could make a dignified withdrawal from a political world she would come to disdain.

Caroline was born on November 27, 1957. Both parents were besotted with their baby daughter; Jack was a doting father, and conveniently that did nothing to harm his political ambitions. His philandering might have, had it reached a wider public. His sexual exploits were common knowledge on Capitol Hill, but newspapers were not interested in a politician's peccadilloes unless they affected his ability to do the job.

Jack was constantly out on the stump, meeting and greeting, raising his profile and broadening his appeal. He wanted to garner votes from north and south, liberals and conservatives, Catholics and non-Catholics, black and white, and he thus nailed few colors to the mast. A notable exception was his work on the McClellan Committee, whose brief was to investigate corruption in the Teamsters Union. By taking on the powerful organization led by Jimmy Hoffa, he showed that he was a man of courage who could play hardball when the situation required. Another area he revisited time and again was foreign affairs; he spoke passionately about the political situation in Southeast Asia and ruffled many feathers with some trenchant views on France's bloody colonial struggle with Algerian nationalists. And then, of course, there was the Red Menace. Jack had long argued that the United States was at a military disadvantage to the Soviet Union, the famous "missile gap." His calculations could be neither proved nor disproved but they certainly struck a chord with many. In all these areas Jack spoke with conviction; holding forth on world affairs risked few votes at home and made him look even more like presidential material.

In 1958, Jack was up for reelection to the Senate, giving him the opportunity to check his progress. He was returned with 73.6 percent of the vote, the largest majority ever recorded in a Massachusetts election. Even before he had publicly declared his candidacy for the 1960 presidential election, the momentum to carry him to the White House seemed unstoppable. By mid-1959, the campaign was in full swing in all but name. A Corvair aircraft, named *Caroline*, was purchased to make his constant crisscrossing of the country easier. It allowed him to reach more Democratic delegates and voters than any potential rival. The outlay was huge, but, of course, that was never an issue. The schedule would have been daunting for a man in peak condition; for Kennedy it was grueling. He had constant back pain, but cortisone injections to keep his adrenal deficiency under control also fleshed out his face and made him even more handsome. Good looks cut little ice with some of the grandees of the Democratic Party, but they underestimated the power of personal appeal. As election year dawned, the Kennedy campaign rolled on like a juggernaut.

First steps on the political ladder

Above: Jack hosts a meeting of campaign workers as he bids to reach the House of Representatives in 1946. After the death of Joe Jr., Kennedy Sr. made Jack's political career his number one priority. When the Congressional seat of Massachusetts' 11th District became vacant, the old stamping ground of both P. J. Kennedy and Honey Fitz, Joe correctly calculated that a name with "Fitzgerald" and "Kennedy" in it, together with almost unlimited resources, would be a winning formula. Jack focused on matters such as employment and housing, with the welfare of war veterans always to the fore. But the main tactic was emotional: he sold himself as a war hero who offered youth and vitality.

Left: Relaxing at Hyannis Port after winning the Democratic nomination as congressman for Massachusetts' 11th District. Because this voting area was overwhelmingly Democratic, the fall election was seen as a formality. On November 5, 1946, Jack comfortably beat his Republican opponent, the beginning of a 14-year journey that would end at the White House.

Socializing and sports

Above: The young congressman relaxes at his apartment in Georgetown, Washington. Initially, he shared the accommodation with his sister Eunice, who worked for the Justice Department. Jack showed little enthusiasm for the day-to-day affairs of government. His chief interests were still socializing and sports, and even allowing for his ongoing back problem, his attendance record in Congress was poor.

Family rocked by further tragedy

Left: May 16, 1948. Less than four years after the death of Joe Jr., the family was struck by another tragedy. Kathleen Kennedy was killed when a plane carrying her and her lover, Lord Fitzwilliam, crashed into a mountain near the town of Privas, France. "Kick" had gone to seek her father's blessing for her proposed marriage to Fitzwilliam. Joe, who was in Europe on a fact-finding tour for the Marshall Plan, was eager to find an accommodation to the problem. Rose was vehemently against the union, because Fitzwilliam was a divorcé. She had previously refused to attend Kick's wedding to Billy Hartington, and she would not attend her daughter's funeral.

Above: August 24, 1949. Twenty-year-old Jacqueline Bouvier (center) and some fellow students head to France for a year-long exchange trip. For Jackie the trip offered an escape from her mother, Janet, who was now Mrs. Hugh Auchinloss. She was also drawn to the country because of her beloved father's Gallic roots.

Opposite: Jack and Franklin Delano Roosevelt Jr., who both took up the cause of war veterans' housing. In his early days on Capitol Hill Jack also served on the Education and Labor Committee, along with a young Republican congressman, Richard Nixon. Jack was non-doctrinaire in his views and he had many Republican friends.

Enter Jackie

Left: After graduating from George Washington University, where she majored in French literature, Jackie moved into journalism. After a brief spell at *Vogue*, she was appointed as the "Inquiring Camera Girl" at the *Washington Times-Herald*. She took up this undemanding job in January 1952. It was while working as a journalist that Jackie befriended Charles Bartlett, at whose house she first met Jack Kennedy.

Below: Bobby Kennedy marries Ethel Skakel at St. Mary's Roman Catholic Church, Greenwich, Connecticut, June 17, 1950, with Eunice Kennedy (left) among the bridesmaids. Ethel had become Jean Kennedy's best friend during their college days at Manhattanville. Jean had played the part of matchmaker, pushing boisterous Ethel and her shy, awkward 20-year-old brother together during a skiing trip to Canada.

Third time Congressman

Above: April 18, 1950. Jack is among a group of congressmen to accept a petition from a contemporary Paul Revere on the steps of the Capitol building. On the 175th anniversary of the famous midnight ride in which Revere warned of the coming of British troops, his latter-day counterpart petitions for home rule for Columbia. In 1950, Jack was returned to Congress for the third time. He deferred to the wishes of his father, who wanted him to run for the Senate in 1952.

Slick campaign the key to Senate election victory

Opposite: Pat and Eunice Kennedy go door-to-door to hand out car bumper stickers and photographs in support of their brother's senatorial campaign. When Joe Kennedy's strident and autocratic management threatened to demoralize the team, Bobby was persuaded to leave his job at the Justice Department and take over the running of the campaign.

Above: Jack's 1952 campaign for the Senate was organized with military efficiency. His opponent for the seat was Henry Cabot Lodge Jr., grandson of the man who had defeated Honey Fitz in 1916. He, too, had looks, charisma, and a fine war record. The difference was Joe Kennedy, who hired the best campaign team money could buy. The PR machine went into overdrive and Jack won by a margin of 70,000 votes. The result was one of the few bright spots for the Democrats in what was a gloomy set of returns. The Republicans were in the ascendancy, both on Capitol Hill and in the White House, where Dwight Eisenhower comfortably defeated Adlai Stevenson. During the campaign Jack's back pain became so acute that he was forced to use crutches. Whenever possible he sought to prevent his health problems from reaching the public domain, so he often dispensed with the crutches just before making his public appearance, but a lengthy session of speechmaking and handshaking sometimes made this impossible.

"Most Eligible Bachelor" announces his engagement

Above: Jackie was well aware of Jack's playboy reputation during their courtship, but it only served to heighten the attraction. She was drawn by the element of danger that he represented, seeing shades of her father in his character and demeanor. Jack was taken by Jackie's cultured ways and witty repartee, as well as her beauty, although he was less than enthusiastic about the commitment of marriage.

Left: Jacqueline Bouvier's elegance and beauty are captured in this 1953 portrait. In January of that year she had attended President Eisenhower's inaugural ball with Jack. Having not seen him for several months after their first meeting in May 1952, Jackie was eager for the romance to progress. She knew the importance of making a good match and was aware that she had failed to "get the ring by spring"—the mantra of her college contemporaries to secure a suitable engagement before graduation.

Opposite: June 1953. The senator and his fiancée leave LaGuardia Airport to spend the weekend at Cape Cod. The engagement had been announced just after the *Saturday Evening Post* ran a feature on Jack as "Washington's Most Eligible Bachelor." It was a moment to savor for Jackie, whose mother had doubted her ability to attract a suitable husband. Jack, meanwhile, had no intention of allowing a marriage certificate to curb his bachelor ways.

A timely marriage

Left: Jack and Jackie, pictured at Hyannis Port two days before their nuptials. Now 35, Jack had realized that his father was right to suggest it was time for him to marry. Jackie intrigued him, he admired her intelligence, and he made the decision that this was enough for him to commit to marriage. The courtship was functional rather than romantic, Jack issuing his proposal by telegram. The Kennedy wealth was certainly an important factor in Jackie's decision to marry. Her father had squandered much of the Bouvier fortune, and when her mother married Hugh Auchinloss, she was surrounded by opulence but was made well aware that she would inherit virtually nothing. She had aristocratic bearing and a family name, but financial security was one of her overriding concerns.

Society wedding of the year

Opposite: September 12, 1953. Jack and Jackie take their vows at the century-old St. Mary's Church in Newport, Rhode Island. Archbishop Richard Cushing, a long-standing family friend, came from Boston to officiate at the service, with Bobby acting as best man.

Left: A huge crowd of well-wishers gathered outside the church. Jackie saw this day as the beginning of married life and was enthused at the prospect of playing an active role in her husband's political career.

Below: Rose Kennedy and Janet Auchinloss engaged in a battle of wills over arrangements for the big day. Janet wanted a restrained affair, but the Kennedys insisted on a lavish celebration. They agreed the Auchinloss house at Hammersmith Farm would provide the backdrop, but new Kennedy money would pay for what would be a media event as well as a wedding.

A disappointment on the day

Left: Jackie's wedding day was marred by the fact that her father did not give her away. Informed by his ex-wife, Janet Auchinloss, that he was not invited to the reception, "Black Jack" got drunk and missed the ceremony. A devastated Jackie had to walk down the aisle on the arm of her stepfather, Hugh Auchinloss. No one dissented from the view that she made a stunning bride, but Jackie herself was less than pleased with her appearance. She disliked the ivory silk taffeta dress that her mother had picked out for her,—the battle between the two thus continued right up until 24-year-old Jackie's wedding day. If Jackie thought that marriage would begin a fresh chapter of undiluted happiness, she was about to be disabused. The luster of the relationship began to wear off as early as the couple's honeymoon in Acapulco.

Last rites administered

Opposite: In October 1954, Jack's back problem became so acute that he was admitted to a New York hospital to undergo a risky double-fusion operation. The recuperation process afforded Jack an excuse to miss a key Senate vote, the censure motion on Senator Joe McCarthy. McCarthy had incurred the wrath of the Senate for his rabid anti-Communist stance and notorious witch hunts for those with "Red" leanings. Jack had sympathy with McCarthy's views, but had to keep one eye on the liberal wing of the party. He could have made his opinion known but avoided the issue.

Below: Jackie is close by as Jack leaves hospital two months after his operation. He had lapsed into a coma and last rites had been administered. When he left hospital, he faced a long recuperation. He had a raw, open wound, and Jackie played an important part in the recovery process, both psychologically and physically. His confinement, and thus his inability to be unfaithful, strengthened their relationship in the short term.

Right: A year into their marriage, the Kennedys present an image of harmony. In fact, it had been a traumatic 12 months. Jackie suffered a miscarriage, which, in a family known for its fecundity, inevitably meant a sense of failure as well as loss. The new Mrs. Kennedy had realized that she was not to play a full supporting role in her husband's political life, and she also found that Jack merely paid lip service to the idea of marital fidelity.

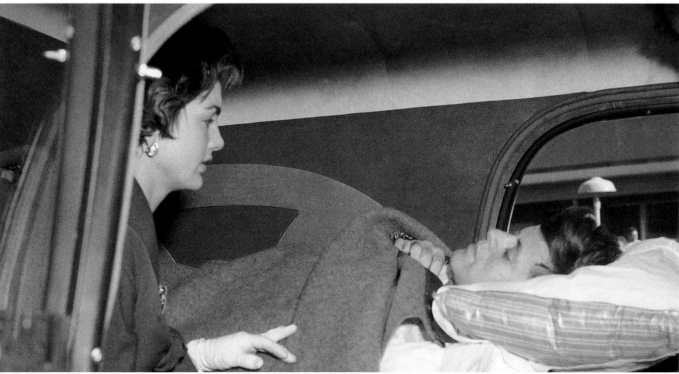

Pulitzer Prize for *Profiles In Courage*

Above: Jack and Jackie enjoy an evening at the Stork Club in May 1955, the month the senator returned to Capitol Hill after his long recuperation from back surgery. He was now being prescribed Novocain and cortisone, and the latter also had the effect of fleshing out his face. The thin, somewhat gaunt look was gone for good, something that appealed to Jack's vanity. During his recovery, Jackie had helped her husband put together ideas for a book about eight senators who had shown outstanding political bravery. It was published early the following year to great acclaim under the title *Profiles In Courage*. The book won a Pulitzer Prize, and enhanced Jack's reputation as a deep political thinker.

Opposite: Jackie tried to embrace the Kennedys' love of competitive sports, but a broken ankle while playing touch football at Cape Cod ended her participation in an activity for which she had no enthusiasm. Jackie called her sisters-in-law the "Rah-Rah Girls" or "Toothy Girls." They dubbed her "The Deb," and took to mimicking her high-pitched voice.

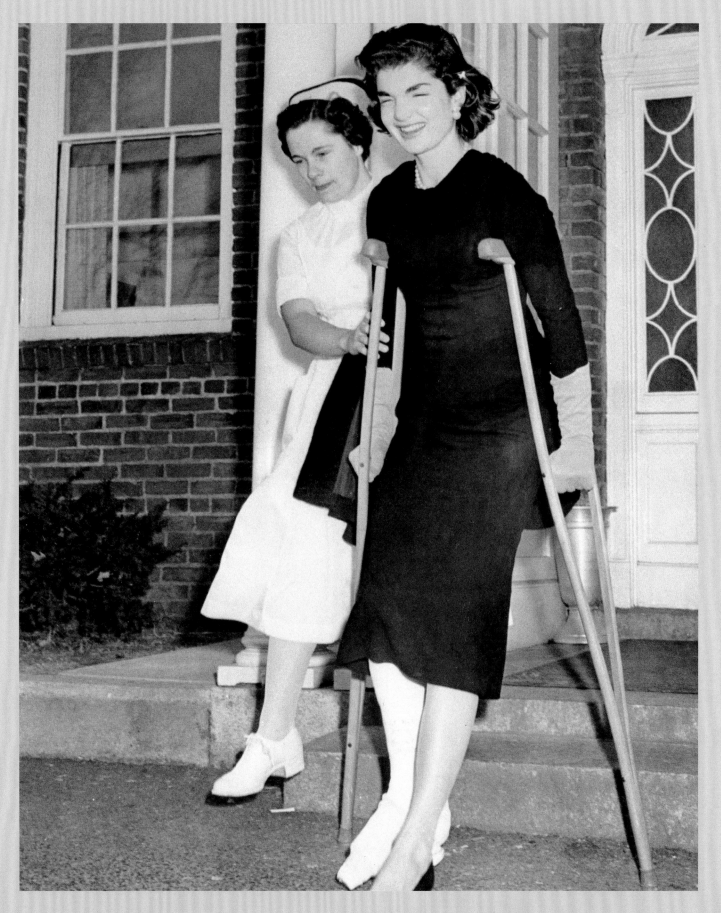

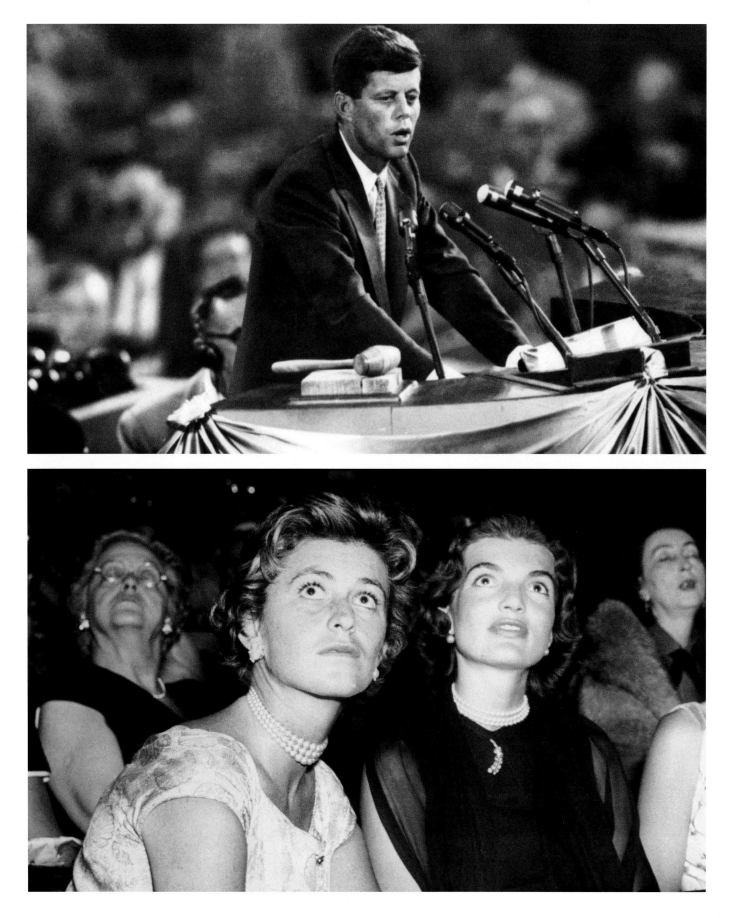

Jack nominates Stevenson for President

Opposite above: August 16, 1956. Jack is widely acclaimed for a barnstorming speech in which he nominated Adlai Stevenson as the Democratic Party's presidential candidate. He went to the Convention insisting he was not a candidate, but let it be known that he would accept the nomination as Stevenson's running mate should it be offered. Stevenson stunned delegates by throwing the choice of vice-president over to the floor, and in the subsequent vote Jack lost out to Estes Kefauver.

Opposite below: Eunice—who had married Robert Shriver in May 1953—and Jackie at the Democratic Convention, Chicago, August 13, 1956. Jackie was eight months' pregnant at the time. Despite the fact that she had already had a miscarriage, Jack headed off to the Mediterranean after the Convention. Jackie was dispatched to Hammersmith Farm to stay with her mother, where she went into premature labor and bore a stillborn child while Jack was on vacation. When he was finally contacted, Jack saw no reason to return home.

Above: Teddy, Jack, and Bobby share a joke in an off-duty moment in 1956. It was a pivotal year for Jack. His failure to secure the vice-presidential nomination turned out to be a blessing in disguise. The Adlai Stevenson–Estes Kefauver ticket was trounced in the November presidential election. Jack's stock had risen during the Convention, yet he remained untainted by the crushing electoral defeat.

Bobby takes on Hoffa

Above: Jack and Bobby in pensive mood during the McClellan Committee hearings in February 1957. Jack served on the committee, which was investigating corruption within labor organizations. Bobby served as Chief Counsel and flourished in a two-year period of painstaking investigative work, particularly his personal duel with Hoffa. Jimmy Hoffa, who succeeded Dave Beck as leader of the powerful Teamsters Union, had been the subject of investigations as early as 1951. Joe Kennedy was wary of taking on such powerful vested interests, and the Democratic Party had traditional links with organized labor. Jack also had reservations, but Bobby was determined to bring legal action against those responsible for corrupt practices. Once the investigations were under way, Jack began to see—and reap—the political benefit of being associated with the committee's crusading work. The McClellan Committee was wound up in 1959. Those under investigation regularly "took the Fifth" and opposition from Republicans on the committee also made it difficult to secure indictments. When Jack became president and Bobby was head of the Justice Department, the two would renew their fight against organized crime.

A new broom

Right: Jack shows off a broom-shaped pin on his lapel, indicating the hopes of the Democratic Party for a "clean sweep" in the 1958 elections. Jack's reelection to the Senate was hardly in doubt, but the family were looking for an overwhelming majority to gain an unstoppable momentum that would carry Jack all the way to the White House. The Kennedys were quick to grasp that the messenger was as important as the message, if not more so. In a country that was accustomed to hard sell, they understood that a presidential candidate could be marketed and sold like any other product.

In the event, Jack took over 73 percent of the vote, the largest majority ever recorded in a Massachusetts election. Jackie played an active role in the campaign, and deliberately toned down her apparel to give the impression that she was in tune with the ordinary voter.

Below: Ethel Kennedy, Jean Smith, and Eunice Shriver look on anxiously as Jack and Bobby continue their probe into union racketeering on the McClellan Committee. Eunice was articulate and politically astute, and only her gender relegated her to a supporting role in the campaign team.

Jackie gives birth to a daughter

Above: After two pregnancies ended in tragedy, Jackie gave birth to a daughter on November 27, 1957. The child was named Caroline Bouvier, after Jackie's sister—whose full name was Caroline Lee—and her father. Black Jack had died from cancer the previous August. Jack was besotted by his daughter, a complete transformation from the indifference he had shown following Jackie's two previous pregnancies. Although fatherhood didn't curb Jack's philandering, it did strengthen the bond between mother and father.

Jackie regarded becoming a mother as the happiest day of her life. It ended all the doubts about her ability to carry a healthy child to term, and it meant that she and Jack now had the bond of parenthood. Jackie tried to protect Caroline from the inevitable media interest, although she did allow *Life* magazine to do a photo shoot in 1958, when Jack was running for reelection to the Senate. Jack was rather more relaxed about using family shots for PR purposes.

Left: Jack and Jackie's leisure interests were quite different. Jackie, an expert horsewoman, loved country pursuits, including hunting. Jack was happiest when he was messing around in boats.

Opposite: Jack and Bobby in Washington, D. C.

CHAPTER THREE

President-Elect 1960

Jack Kennedy formally announced his candidacy on January 2, 1960. The themes of his address were the arms race and the Soviet threat, managing the newly emerging nations, and creating conditions for prosperity at home. A moral imperative would inform all policy matters in a Kennedy administration. It was motherhood and apple pie, nothing to take exception to. He entered several primaries, hoping to overwhelm potential rivals. Chief rival was Hubert Humphrey; the Minnesota senator went head-to-head with Jack in the Wisconsin primary, and quickly felt the full force of the Kennedy machine. He had meager resources, not to mention a less glamorous consort. Jackie played the role of dutiful candidate's wife to the full, and the pair worked the crowds like Hollywood stars. Pregnancy would soon force Jackie to take a back seat, something which, no doubt, she was not too unhappy about.

Jack won in Wisconsin, taking 40 percent of the popular vote. He and Humphrey then moved on to West Virginia, which would prove to be decisive as far as the latter's chances were concerned. Religion quickly emerged as a key issue; there were undoubtedly voters who would find it difficult to stomach a Catholic in the White House. Jack went on the offensive, stressing his view that a clear line be drawn between church and state—religious beliefs would play no part when it came to making policy. The trump card was his and his elder brother's wartime service. He pointed out that Uncle Sam hadn't been interested in their religion when the two of them had gone into battle. It

was a persuasive argument, and had the secondary effect of bringing Humphrey's war record into play—he had been unfit for active service. It was all perfectly genuine, but it looked poor next to the resumé of a decorated war hero. It also became clear that some of Humphrey's natural supporters switched sides merely to avoid being labeled bigots. Others disregarded the issue altogether, having had a positive experience of Catholics in positions of political power over many years.

The Kennedys left nothing to chance. Franklin Delano Roosevelt Jr. was brought into the campaign team, a clever move that gave the illusion that one of the hallowed names in U.S. political history was supporting the Kennedy campaign. Eleanor Roosevelt herself had no time for Kennedy; she once famously remarked that he often showed "too much profile and not enough courage." Issues such as the McCarthy censure motion and civil rights had prompted the former First Lady's acidic comment, turning the Pulitzer Prize-winning work back on its author.

However, the mood of the majority in West Virginia was clear: here was a man who could prevent the Republicans from making it three victories in presidential elections. Jack carried the state by 219,000 to 142,000 votes, taking 61 percent of the popular vote. Humphrey withdrew from the race, pointing to the amount of money that his opponent was able to throw at the campaign as the decisive factor. It later emerged that some of those vast resources were used for dubious purposes. Large donations were made to Protestant ministers, and years later some openly admitted that this thinly veiled bribery had had the desired effect on the ballot box.

Opposite: Jackie put aside her disdain for politics to play an active role in the campaign until pregnancy forced her to take a back seat. During the primaries, the "Jackie factor" contributed to Humphrey's defeat.

Meanwhile, Kennedy found time for affairs, despite the intense media scrutiny he was under as the front-running candidate. His liaison with Judith Campbell was potentially the most explosive; they met in March 1960, brought together by Frank Sinatra. The entertainer also introduced Campbell to Mafia boss Sam Giancana, but instead of recoiling at the prospect of sharing a mistress with a mobster, Jack seemed to welcome it. He persuaded Campbell to arrange a meeting between him and Giancana in April, after which the Mafia were heavily involved in getting the Kennedy vote out by any means at their disposal. Giancana was undoubtedly seeking influence at the highest level and an accommodation on federal probes into Mafia business.

Below: Jack and Bobby talk tactics before the Democratic convention. The two worked in tandem when the civil rights issue threatened to derail the campaign. Jack made all the right liberal noises in public, while Bobby wooed Southern delegates behind the scenes.

It soon became difficult to see beyond Kennedy as the Democratic presidential candidate. He comfortably prevailed in several other primaries, and the more he looked like a winner, the more the voters swung behind him. By July 1960, when Los Angeles hosted the Democratic Convention, there seemed to be only one final hurdle to overcome, after Lyndon Johnson belatedly threw his hat into the ring. The veteran Senate majority leader had greater experience, making a major contribution to the legislative program, while his opponent had busied himself on peripheral matters, if he bothered to turn up at all. Jack responded by making a virtue of his youth and vitality—an obvious sideswipe at the major heart attack Johnson had suffered five years earlier. In turn, Johnson's camp brought up Jack's continuing health problems. It all threatened to get nasty.

Jack's hard-line anti-Communist stance had kept the conservatives on board, but he needed to boost his liberal

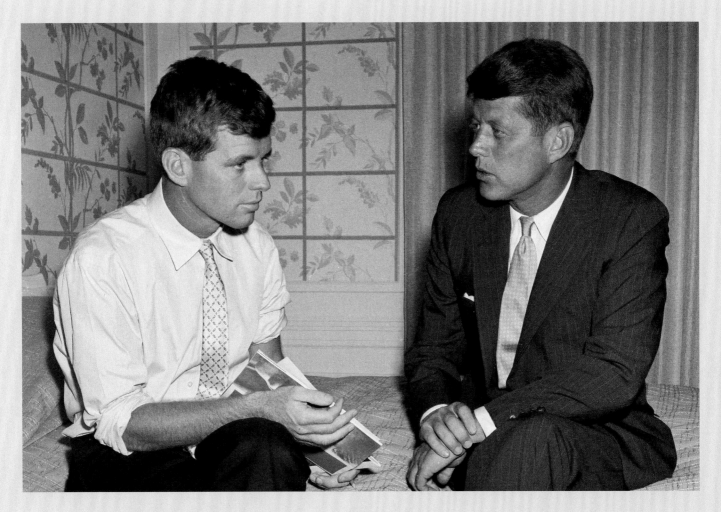

credentials and the civil rights issue gave him the perfect platform. He hadn't been outspoken on the subject until now, but in the final days before the vote he went into overdrive. Johnson challenged Jack to a television debate, where he hoped his greater experience would give him the edge. But Jack was too wily; he kept on safe ground and spoke in broad generalities, and it proved inconclusive.

Jack won the nomination on the first ballot, with 806 votes to Johnson's 409. Despite the animosity between the two men, Jack chose Johnson as his running mate, a decision that initially shocked his campaign team. It was pragmatic on both sides; Jack knew the Texas man on the ticket would help in the vital Southern states. He also thought it better to have Johnson on board than as a hostile outsider. Johnson wanted the top job, and is said to have reached his decision after counting up the number of presidents who had died in office. In his acceptance speech Jack spoke of the "new frontier," with echoes of Roosevelt's famous New Deal nearly 30 years earlier. He said: "There are new frontiers for America to conquer, in education, in science, in national purpose. Not frontiers on a map, but frontiers of the mind, the will, the spirit of man."

The man who stood between Jack and the White House was Eisenhower's vice-president, Richard Nixon. Eisenhower's legacy was prosperity at home and peace abroad, and Nixon began the campaign ahead in the polls. After Congress was adjourned on September 1, Jack hit the ground running—over the next two months he made countless five-minute speeches, with overcoming inertia as a recurring theme. He would get the United States moving again, moving forward. The religious question came up again; Nixon wanted it off the agenda, but Jack saw the value of raising the issue in order to dismiss it.

The highlight of the whole campaign was a series of four televised debates between candidates. The first, on September 26, proved to be the watershed. The content was unremarkable, but the camera loved Jack, while Nixon looked ill at ease. Those who listened on radio found Nixon's authoritative, resonant voice more appealing, and felt he got the better of the exchanges. However, they were in a minority compared to the 70 million who had the pictures to go with the words. Afterward, when Kennedy was out on the stump, he was mobbed like a movie star—his looks and charisma were major factors in determining the outcome of the election.

An event that would have allowed Nixon to turn things around before polling day did occur, but he failed to take advantage. It concerned Martin Luther King Jr., the 31-year-old head of the Southern Christian Leadership Conference and the most prominent black leader in the country. King was jailed on October 19 for taking part in a sit-in in Atlanta, protesting about the city's segregationist practices. A trumped-up driving charge was added and he was sentenced to four months. While Nixon wavered, Jack make a direct call to King's wife, Coretta, expressing his concern. Bobby made representations to the judge, and King was soon released. King had been a lukewarm Kennedy supporter before the incident; now he openly endorsed the Democratic candidate, and at a stroke virtually assured Jack of carrying the majority black vote. One of those was King's own father, an avowed Republican.

In the event it proved to be a very close-run thing. More than 68 million votes were cast, the biggest turnout in the country's history. Just 112,000 votes separated the candidates, the closest result since 1884. The margin of victory in the Electoral College was more decisive, Kennedy securing 303 votes to Nixon's 220. On the morning of November 9, John Fitzgerald Kennedy made his acceptance speech at Hyannis Port Armory. At 43, he was the youngest-ever elected president and the first Catholic incumbent. The election machine had done its job; it was now time to see what Kennedy would deliver in office.

First there was a family celebration; on November 25 Jackie gave birth to their second child. Jack missed the birth yet again; he was en route to Florida when he learned Jackie had been taken to hospital and made every effort to return to Washington in time, but John F. Kennedy Jr. had already been delivered by Cesarean section. If Jackie entertained hopes that fatherhood the second time around and the responsibilities of office would put a brake on Jack's tendency to wander, she was to be sorely disappointed.

SENATOR JOHN F. KENNEDY
PRESIDENTIAL CANDIDATE

Cronkite interviews the declared candidate

Above: Legendary CBS news anchorman Walter Cronkite prepares to interview Kennedy. Jack formally declared that he was running for president on January 2, 1960, although in reality he had been campaigning nonstop since the Senate elections of 1958. It was the start of the year that would be the culmination of a 14-year journey since Kennedy entered politics. For his father it would be the realization of a dream. Cronkite raised the Catholic issue during the discussion, despite an agreement that religion was to be off limits.

Left: Jack soon realized that his looks and style were perfectly suited to television.

Opposite: Jackie and Caroline wait for Jack to fulfill yet another speaking engagement. Jackie was portrayed as a full-time mother, yet she employed a live-in nurse to cater for Caroline's everyday needs. Jack's political opponents bemoaned the effect that both Jackie and Caroline had on public opinion. The candidate encouraged family photo opportunities to capitalize on the fact. He named the Corvair aircraft purchased for electioneering purposes after his daughter.

Kennedy targets primaries

Left: All the Kennedy family were mobilized during the campaign. Here, Jack stops off to see his sister, Patricia Lawford, who had three children under five at the time of the election.

Despite his obvious appeal, Jack faced three major handicaps in winning the Democratic presidential nomination. He was young and relatively inexperienced, especially compared with Lyndon Johnson, who was seen as a likely rival; accusations were still rife that he was not his own man but a mere pawn acting out his father's own thwarted ambitions; and there was the issue of his faith, no Roman Catholic ever having been elected as chief executive of the United States. Many senior figures in the Democratic Party, including Harry Truman and Eleanor Roosevelt, thought that Kennedy had too much image and too little substance. They underestimated the power of personal appeal and charisma, which Kennedy had in abundance. Jack made the decision to enter several primaries, hoping to build up momentum in his bid to become the Democratic presidential candidate. He carried New Hampshire comfortably.

Brothers in arms

Opposite below: Twenty-eight-year-old Teddy Kennedy (right) was assigned 13 western states during the campaign. His penchant for daredevil stunts had more impact than his oratory, as Nixon fared much better than Kennedy in this territory.

Above: Thirty-four-year-old Bobby Kennedy was a much more potent figure in the election, a singleminded political fixer who proved to be the ideal person to lead the backroom team—the *éminence grise* behind the scenes. He was ruthlessly efficient, determined to do whatever it took to get his brother elected. As a taskmaster he was as hard on himself as he was on others. He didn't just remain at the nerve center of the campaign, but took on a grueling schedule of meetings in the Midwest, often in atrocious weather conditions.

Humphrey's hopes ended

Left: Jack and Jackie at Idlewild Airport, New York. Jack took 61 percent of the popular vote in Charleston, West Virginia, effectively ending Hubert Humphrey's chances of securing the Democratic nomination.

Below: Jack attends the 309th commencement of Harvard University. He was a Harvard alumnus himself, graduating *cum laude* in political science in 1940.

Opposite above: Jack is guest of honor at the Massachusetts Pre-Preliminary Convention dinner in Boston. State Secretary Joseph Ward, Congressman Francis O'Neill, and Lt. Governor Robert Murphy greet the front-running candidate enthusiastically. As Kennedy prevailed in primary after primary, Democrats increasingly swung behind his campaign, eager to be associated with a winner.

Opposite below: Jack keeps the voters and cameramen happy at International Airport, Los Angeles. As he crisscrossed the country, he mastered the art of delivering short, punchy speeches on a range of subjects. His speed-reading, combined with the ability to memorize huge amounts of data, helped him enormously during campaigning.

"Rocked to political lullabies..."

Right: Jackie remained at Hyannis Port instead of attending the Democratic Convention, which opened on July 11 in Los Angeles. She was carefully primed during the campaign—she was warned about being drawn on any issue in public, and even smoking was forbidden. Her impact was significant. She was the epitome of glamour and style, and countless column inches were devoted to her appearance.

Below: In Jackie's absence, Rose Kennedy occupies the seat next to her son and his running mate at the Democratic Convention. Rose articulated her son's credentials by commenting that he "was rocked to political lullabies."

Kennedy fails to win over former First Lady

Right: There is a palpably frosty air as Eleanor Roosevelt exchanges words with Kennedy at the Democratic Convention. The former First Lady was unimpressed by Jack's liberal credentials, and would have supported Adlai Stevenson if the twice-defeated candidate had chosen to run.

Below: Kennedy with Frank Sinatra at a fund-raiser on the eve of his selection as the Democratic presidential candidate. Kennedy loved the Hollywood glitz that the entertainer and his coterie represented. It was Sinatra who introduced Jack to Judith Campbell, a mistress he shared with mobster Sam Giancana. "High Hopes," Sinatra's famous song, became an apposite campaign anthem. However, he would come to be regarded as a liability, and the Kennedys eventually severed all relations with the crooner.

Smiles hide animosity between Kennedy and Johnson

Above: Lyndon Johnson applauds as Kennedy steps up to speak to the Texas Delegation during the Democratic Convention. Notwithstanding his success in the primaries, Jack still had to secure the endorsement of his party. Johnson played a waiting game. The Senate Leader hadn't entered the primaries, but felt he could still win the nomination. Exchanges between the two camps before the declarations were vitriolic. Kennedy prevailed on the first ballot, with 808 votes to Johnson's 409. Despite the animosity between the two men, Kennedy asked Johnson to be his running mate. The invitation was given—and accepted—for political purposes.

Left: Bobby takes soundings on the floor of the Convention hall. He is pictured talking to his brother-in-law, actor Peter Lawford, who married Patricia Kennedy in 1954. Lawford was a conduit for Jack's extracurricular activities, organizing parties and providing a steady supply of girls.

Civil rights question

Above: Wisconsin delegate Vel Phillips questions the candidate about his commitment to civil rights. Kennedy frustrated black leaders with his refusal to give a firm policy pledge on the issue. This returned to haunt him during his administration, and it would not be until after his death that legislation was finally enacted.

Jackie welcomes home the candidate

Above: Having spent the week of the Convention in an almost deserted Kennedy compound, Jackie welcomes Jack back to Hyannis Port amid tumultuous scenes. In his absence she worked on a painting depicting Jack as Napoleon, with "Il Senatore" inscribed on a three-cornered hat. She presented it to him as a gift to celebrate winning the presidential nomination.

Opposite below: Bobby Kennedy Jr. explains the mysteries of flight to his Uncle Jack as family members return to Boston following the party Convention.

Opposite above: Missouri senator Stuart Symington was one of the contenders for the Democratic presidential nomination, numbering former president Harry Truman among his supporters. He lacked charisma, however, and came third in the ballot, a long way behind both Kennedy and Johnson. Here, he congratulates the worthy victor by holding aloft a copy of the *Detroit Times*.

Bobby demands unity in New York

Opposite above: Feuding Democrats in New York bring Bobby to the city on a peace mission. Here, he discusses the possibility of a temporary truce with Mayor Robert Wagner on the steps of his official residence, Gracie Mansion. Jack knew he had to have a broad appeal if he was to win. He targeted young voters and factory workers in the industrial heartlands of the Northeast. With Johnson on the ticket, the Democrats hoped for a strong showing in the South. In particular, it was vital to win back Texas and Louisiana, and hold the Carolinas.

Opposite below: August 7, 1960. Jack and Jackie onboard their sailing boat *Wianno Senior*. Jack returned to Washington the following day, and began the task of eating into the Republican lead in the polls.

Above: Jack and Bobby confer prior to a controversial Senate vote on medical care for seniors. The issue remained unresolved when Congress was adjourned a week later, September 1, 1960.

Journalists ignore Kennedy's womanizing

Above: An off-duty family photograph taken at Cape Cod, just before Jack hit the campaign trail.

Right: Jackie embraces her husband in a touching, unposed moment captured through a car window. Jack's infidelity was common knowledge in Washington, but journalists were not interested in the candidate's private peccadilloes.

Opposite: Jackie, pictured at the couple's Georgetown home. She put her creative talents to work in refurbishing their first permanent home, angering her notoriously parsimonious husband.

In the public eye

Opposite: The family share a quiet moment at Hyannis Port. Despite her wish to support Jack's campaign, Jackie hated the intrusion and loss of privacy that it inevitably brought. Shortly after he won the nomination, she ordered extra fencing to be erected at the "Kennedy Compound" in Hyannis Port, hoping to deter the hordes of sightseers.

Above: Jack goes over his notes before giving yet another address. The combination of his oratorical skills and Ted Sorensen's speech-writing was a powerful campaigning weapon.

United front

Above: Bobby Kennedy and Lyndon Johnson show a united front—in public, at least. Privately, Bobby was left fuming at the choice of Johnson as running mate. The Senate majority leader had little time for Bobby, whom he considered a young upstart. Johnson's wife, Lady Bird, also had great reservations about her husband agreeing to run as vice-president.

Left: September 3, 1960. A two-hour stop in San Francisco en route to Anchorage is more than enough time to deliver another barnstorming speech. Jack spoke of the New Frontier and Moving Ahead, which would be recurring campaign themes.

Opposite: A moment of quiet reflection during two months of intense politicking. Kennedy toured the country at breakneck speed, visiting far more cities than his Republican opponent.

Kennedy turns Catholic issue to his advantage

Opposite above and below: The Kennedys attend a $100-a-plate fund-raiser in Washington to boost party coffers. Jack made his first nationwide television address at the function. The issue of his Catholicism was in the spotlight at this point. Far from being a potential vote loser, the issue became a positive boon to the Kennedy campaign. In the end it was Nixon who wanted to bury the religious question, while Jack was happy to keep it alive.

Above: Because Jackie was in the latter stages of pregnancy, she was unable to keep up with her husband's exhausting schedule. A reception at the Hotel Commodore, New York, in mid-September was one of the few times they were able to appear together.

Head to head with Nixon

Left: Kennedy and Nixon observe the social niceties before the first of their four televised debates (below and opposite). Jack was only four years younger than his Republican rival, but the image gap was much wider. He would be the first White House incumbent to be born in the twentieth century.

Nixon believed he would get the better of Kennedy in these exchanges. In terms of scoring points the debates were largely inconclusive. However, while Nixon looked nervous and ill at ease, Jack's good looks and charisma made a favorable impression on the voters.

The debates were more noteworthy for the perceptions they created than the merit of the candidates' arguments. The minority who listened on radio thought that Nixon had the edge. However, there were now more than 40 million television sets in the United States, and the vast majority saw a Republican candidate who looked nervous and unhealthy. After the first encounter, Jack was mobbed like a movie star, while Nixon's own mother telephoned to ask if her son was unwell.

Jackie on the campaign trail

Left: Jackie meets Katherine Ellickson of the Women's Committee for New Frontier. This was one of several meetings with officials whose expertise was in social policy, and was no doubt used to help counter the view that Jackie, with her cultured ways and expensive tastes, lacked the common touch. Jackie also hosted a number of parties at the Kennedys' Washington home.

Below: With three weeks still to go before the election, the Kennedys enjoy a ticker-tape reception in Manhattan. This was Jackie's last campaign appearance with her husband.

Opposite: Jackie holds a press conference at her Washington home. Public speaking was not her forte, and she could be abrasive in such situations.

The President-elect and the family man

Above: Jack enjoys a brief respite from his grueling schedule to spend some time with Jackie and Caroline. Jack found it easy to reconcile his role as husband and father with his need for casual sex. He was capable of great tenderness and affection where his family was concerned, yet within minutes of being separated from them he could be cavorting with another woman. He saw this as a compartmentalized need rather than a betrayal.

Right: Jackie and Claudia "Lady Bird" Johnson. It was all smiles for the camera, but Lady Bird wept when she learned that her husband had agreed to run for vice-president. The two women were not close, but did share an unwavering support for their husbands' careers. Lady Bird was an experienced political wife and carried off the role with aplomb. When Jackie's pregnancy curtailed her ability to campaign, Lady Bird stepped up her own commitments to compensate.

A heavy schedule

Above: Jack's heavy campaigning schedule meant that he was an absent father for long periods. It is said that "airplane" was among the first words Caroline Kennedy uttered.

Things were now going well for the Democrats. The TV debates had turned the deficit into a three-point lead for Kennedy. Nixon also blundered when Martin Luther King Jr. was jailed during a protest in Atlanta. While he vacillated, Kennedy acted, expediting King's release. This was a turning point in securing the crucial black vote, although when Americans went to the polls on November 8, the result was still too close to call.

Kennedys out in force to celebrate victory

Above: Eunice, Patricia, and Ethel show a mixture of happiness and relief as the tide of the election results starts to turn in Jack's favor.

Opposite above: With just 24 hours to go before voting begins, Jack prepares to make a final network TV broadcast. New Hampshire is the venue, and Governor Luther Hodges hosts the proceedings. Eunice, Jean, and Pat are on hand to offer their support, while Bobby gives his final words of advice over the phone. After the election, Kennedy would appoint 62-year-old Hodges as Secretary for Commerce, making him the oldest man in the new administration.

Opposite below: The Kennedy clan come out in force as Jack makes his victory speech at Hyannis Port Armory on November 9. Unlike the rest of the family, Joe had been deliberately kept out of the limelight during the campaign. There had been concern that the Republicans would make political capital out of the suggestion that Jack was merely his father's puppet.

The moment of victory

Left: Hyannis Port, November 10, 1960.
After an exhaustive concerted effort, the
Kennedy clan are able to relax and savor the
moment of victory. Standing (left to right):
Ethel Kennedy, Stephen Smith, Jean Kennedy
Smith, the President-elect, Bobby Kennedy,
Patricia Kennedy Lawford, Sargent Shriver, Joan
Kennedy, and Peter Lawford. Seated (left to
right): Eunice Kennedy, Rose Kennedy, Joseph
Kennedy, Jackie, and Teddy Kennedy. Jackie got
on well with her father-in-law, perhaps seeing
shades of her own father in him. Her relationship
with Rose was much more strained at this point.

Fatherhood second time round

Opposite: John F. Kennedy Jr. after his christening at the Georgetown University hospital chapel. Jack was onboard *Caroline* bound for Florida when he received word that Jackie had gone into labor and been rushed into hospital. John F. Kennedy Jr. was born by Cesarean section before Jack could return to Washington.

Left: The President names the new Attorney General on the front steps of his Georgetown home. Both men were concerned that the fact that Bobby had no legal training would bring forth accusations of nepotism. Ironically, it was younger brother Teddy who was the law student. It wouldn't be long before the family would turn its efforts toward helping Teddy forge a political career.

Below: Kennedy and Nixon shake hands for the cameras as they meet in Florida a week after the election. The official return gave Kennedy 34,227,096 votes to Nixon's 34,108,546. Such a narrow margin, together with rumors of ballot rigging, prompted Nixon's aides to demand a recount in some of the states where the result had been closest. Nixon refused. He didn't want to be labeled an ungracious loser, something that might have affected his chances in any future bid to reach the White House. Although he chose not to challenge the result, Nixon was undoubtedly aggrieved. He arranged to have his speech conceding defeat read for him, prompting Jack to remark: "He went out the way he came in—no class."

CHAPTER FOUR

The New Frontier 1961

JFK's inauguration took place on January 20, 1961. It was a bright but bitterly cold day, yet Jack, true to the image of robust vitality he had fostered, braved the ceremony without hat or overcoat. Also typically, the outward appearance didn't tell the whole story, for Jack took the precaution of wearing thermal underwear.

Jack wanted the proceedings to be imbued with cultural as well as political significance. Robert Frost, one of the country's most distinguished men of letters, was invited to read a piece composed specially for the occasion. Its theme was hope and optimism, with the country about to enter a golden age of poetry and power. The blinding sunlight meant that Frost was unable to read the piece, which was to be a preface to an earlier work. He recited that poem from memory instead. It contained the line "Such as we were we gave ourselves outright," which was supremely apposite for the occasion.

At 12:51 Chief Justice Earl Warren administered the oath, and JFK was sworn in to preside over an administration that was to last 1,037 days. The inaugural address was a masterpiece of rhetoric and delivery. It had gone through countless drafts over many weeks. Jack was the overseer, honing and tweaking, but as ever the mastermind was Sorensen. It paid due respect to the country's heritage and proud traditions, but its central theme was moving forward. The future would bring many challenges, "the common enemies of man: tyranny, poverty, disease, and war itself." The struggle against these evils and the defense of freedoms the country held so dear would come at a

Left: September 1961. The President and First Lady attend mass at St. Francis Xavier, Hyannis, where many of the Kennedy family services were held.

price, however, and sacrifice would be needed. "And so, my fellow Americans, ask not what your country can do for you—ask what you can do for your country." The emphasis on global rather than domestic issues was deliberate, and presaged the amount of time and energy the new President would devote to foreign affairs.

Kennedy had referred to "a new generation of Americans" in his address, and his program was called the New Frontier. However, his first executive decisions were firmly rooted in the past. He reappointed J. Edgar Hoover and Allen Dulles as head of the FBI and CIA, respectively, to the dismay of many of his supporters. Kennedy liked to surround himself with liberal intellectuals, such as J. K. Galbraith, but when it came to making appointments, he valued those who could act as well as think. Hoover and Dulles were almost national institutions; besides, they were in possession of much sensitive information, such as that about Jack's adulterous behavior and the unvarnished truth about his wartime exploits. It made sense to have them on board.

Dean Rusk, a Rhodes scholar and head of the Rockefeller Foundation, was appointed Secretary of State. Robert McNamara was given the defense portfolio. McNamara had recently been appointed head of the Ford Motor Company. A Phi Beta Kappa graduate of the University of California, he was a deep thinker as well as an outstanding businessman. For the sensitive Treasury job, Jack again played safe and decided on C. Douglas Dillon, the undersecretary in the outgoing administration. Jack was more interested that those surrounding him should be high achievers than—in McNamara's and Dillon's case— whether they had Republican leanings. Indeed, most of his appointments were conservative, and they embraced bipartisanship. They did little for the civil rights movement, however; no black was given any senior post in the administration.

The most controversial decision was handing the attorney generalship to 34-year-old Bobby. To install someone who hadn't studied law as head of the Justice Department, with its 30,000-strong staff, was bound to invite charges of nepotism. Bobby had been reluctant to accept at first, relenting only after Jack reiterated his need to have someone absolutely trustworthy in that key position. Another Kennedy prominent in Jack's administration, though without a portfolio, was his father. Joe had melted into the background during the campaign to avoid allegations that a vote for Jack was a vote for the elder Kennedy. Now it was perfectly safe for Joe to return to the stage, and the two had been in regular contact.

Kennedy's men were the brightest and best. Even so, Jack by instinct and inclination was no committee man or easy delegator. He intended to assume the role of chief executive in the fullest sense of the word. He was also much more concerned with tackling immediate issues than long-term strategic planning. It wouldn't be long before he got the opportunity to make some decisions of global significance.

Kennedy's first State of the Union address, on January 30, 1961, was solemn in tone. The dangers posed by the Cold War were highlighted by the fact that Communism had established a foothold just 90 miles from American soil, in Castro's Cuba. Jack was acutely aware that Cuba was one of several potential flashpoints where there was potential for conflict between East and West. Nikita Khrushchev,

Below: The President-elect at the Miami Orange Bowl, January, 1961.

while congratulating Kennedy on his election victory, also made it clear that the Soviet Union stood foursquare behind any insurgents who sought to liberate their country from capitalist imperialists. Communism would spread through a succession of wars of liberation in the Third World. Jack, a firm believer in the Domino Theory, took this threat very seriously. He had two responses to it; the first was open and diplomatic, the second covert and militaristic.

The diplomatic initiatives were the Peace Corps and the Alliance For Progress. The former, which was established on March 1, involved sending teams of highly skilled volunteers to developing countries to help them tackle economic and social problems. The latter was aimed specifically at Latin American countries, helping them to improve standards in health and education, and achieve economic stability. Both initiatives had noble aims, but the secondary objective was not hard to discern: the administration wanted to attack the conditions that could all too easily create revolutionary zealots.

If diplomatic initiatives failed to secure stable, anti-Communist buffer zones, there remained the military option. And as far as Cuba was concerned, it was already too late for diplomacy. Jack had inherited a CIA operation in which anti-Castro Cuban exiles were being trained and equipped in Guatemala. The objective of Operation Pluto was for this 1,500-strong force to ignite a widespread uprising on the island, and topple its Marxist government. Running in tandem was a separate plot in which the help of Mafia bosses was enlisted for an assassination attempt on the Cuban leader. Eisenhower may not have known about the involvement of mobsters; given that Sam Giancana was one of those consulted, it is barely conceivable that Kennedy didn't know, and approve, of this course of action. In the event, two attempts were made on Castro's life before the invasion took place.

On April 15, following a preliminary air strike by six B-26 bombers, Kennedy gave the green light for the invasion to go ahead. Against the wishes of military chiefs, it was decided that the Bay of Pigs would be the landing site. It was swampy terrain, 100 miles west of Trinidad. Castro was already on full alert. The planned invasion was virtually common knowledge; only the time and place remained unknown. The air strike made no serious dent in Castro's arsenal, but it did remove the element of surprise. When the invading force landed in the early hours of Monday, April 17, the whole plan quickly unraveled. Jack was in a quandary; he was naturally drawn to the idea of an audacious raid, but he was desperate to preserve the fiction that the exiles were acting alone. He wasn't helped by the fact that both hawks and doves were vying for his ear. CIA Deputy Director Richard Bissell, the plan's architect, emphasized the importance of decisive, prompt action. Dean Rusk and Arthur Schlesinger Jr. were among those who thought the enterprise flawed.

Jack canceled a second air strike, which was to have provided cover while the invading force established a beachhead. Cuban aircraft thus met with no resistance as they sank two supply ships. The invaders were quickly overwhelmed, with 114 killed and 1,189 captured. Jack was devastated at the news of such an ignominious defeat.

He made a brave fist of it. In the wake of the debacle he remained combative, committed to the fight against Communism on the United States' doorstep. He also assumed total responsibility for the enterprise, something that helped to preserve his popularity. Privately, he was seething, feeling he had been misled into thinking it was a high-reward, low-risk operation.

Negotiations began to free the captives. A deal was eventually struck for their release, the United States paying some $56 million in cash and goods. It was condemned by some as tantamount to the United States yielding to blackmail. However, with the threat of trial and execution hanging over the captives' heads, many heaped praise on Kennedy for his statesmanlike behavior and compassion. On December 29, a rally was held at Miami's Orange Bowl to celebrate the captives' release. Jack was in upbeat mood, stressing that the Bay of Pigs represented only a temporary reversal. By then a new plan was in place: Operation Mongoose. The aim remained the same, but this time it would be achieved by stealth and infiltration. Propaganda and sabotage would be the main weapons in destabilizing the Castro regime and ultimately removing its leader.

Two more theaters of potential East–West conflict provided Kennedy with food for thought in the early days of his presidency: Southeast Asia and Berlin. Since the defeat of the French at Dien Bien Phu in 1954, the United States had strongly supported South Vietnam's non-Communist regime, headed by Ngo Dinh Diem. By mid-1961, Diem's government was very unpopular and looked a prime target for forces from the Communist North. Kennedy sent Johnson to Saigon to assess the situation, and the Vice President reported back suggesting a major U.S. deployment in the area. Kennedy balked at the idea. With the Bay of Pigs fiasco fresh in his memory—and that with Cuba just 90 miles away—he was circumspect about fighting a war thousands of miles from home, so he opted for a huge increase in aid to prop up Diem's ailing regime.

An even more immediate problem was Laos. Pathet Lao guerrilla forces, with backing from Hanoi and Moscow, were making inroads in a country that Kennedy, like Eisenhower before him, regarded as a strategic bulwark against Communism. By the time Kennedy came face to face with Khrushchev in Vienna, in June 1961, there was an uneasy cease-fire in Laos. The two leaders reaffirmed their desire to end hostilities in the country, although this would prove to be a temporary respite.

In late May 1961, the Kennedys embarked on a state visit to Europe. For Jackie, the first six months of the presidency had revolved around organizing the refurbishment of the White House. Her plans to replace poor reproductions with period pieces quickly consumed the government funds allocated, and became another cause of friction with her notoriously parsimonious husband. Clothes were another passion for the First Lady. She had appointed Oleg Cassini as her official designer, and he had been the inspiration behind the woolen coat and pillbox hat worn by Jackie at the Inauguration and much copied thereafter. Jackie dazzled during the first leg of the European visit to France. Jack, noting the impact his chic and beautiful wife had on the crowds, quipped that he was "the man who accompanied Jackie Kennedy to Paris."

JFK's talks with Charles de Gaulle were cordial. The two agreed that any Soviet action that threatened West Berlin's status had to be resisted. Speaking from bitter experience, France's president also cautioned Kennedy about military involvement in Southeast Asia.

The Kennedys went on to Vienna, where Jack had a torrid time in his two-day summit with Khrushchev. There was agreement that Laos should be neutral, but frosty exchanges over West Berlin. Kennedy reiterated that the United States would go to any lengths to defend the status quo. Khrushchev talked of signing a treaty with East Germany, a clear threat to NATO forces in the divided city. The potential escalation was made more worrying by the lack of agreement over nuclear testing. Kennedy had been put on the back foot as he headed for Britain and a meeting with Prime Minister Harold Macmillan. It didn't help that he was suffering severe back pain at the time, for which he was taking amphetamines—substances that were known to impair judgment.

On August 13, there was a dramatic turn of events. East Germany, desperate to stem the flow of defections to West Berlin, which was running at thousands per day, began to construct a wall across the city. West Germany looked to Kennedy for an immediate and strong response. He opted for a more measured reaction, ordering a convoy of 1,500 troops on a 110-mile journey from West Germany along the autobahn into West Berlin. They arrived unhindered. Ironically, after the initial posturing, the building of the Wall eased East–West tensions. Khrushchev didn't sign the treaty with East Germany, and West Berlin remained open.

By now, the "Hundred Days of Action" had long since elapsed—and with the exception of the founding of the Peace Corps, the early months accomplished little of substance. One notable area of inactivity was on the issue of civil rights. The battle to end discrimination should have sat comfortably on the agenda of a Democratic president, and high on it, too. During the election campaign Jack had spoken of ending segregation in federal housing "at the stroke of the pen." Yet, even this small matter remained unaddressed at the end of 1961. The lack of action disappointed liberals seeking major reforms, and in May 1961 two busloads representing the Congress of Racial Equality decided to take matters into their own hands.

Above: January 1961. The first family returns to Washington.

Dubbed "Freedom Riders," they drove into Mississippi and Alabama to protest against segregation. There were ugly scenes, and federal marshals were deployed to restore order. Bobby was sent as peacemaker; he exhorted black leaders to seek redress through the ballot box instead of demonstrations. He also called on the transport industry for an end to segregation in bus, rail, and air travel. The black population was unimpressed at such half-hearted measures, and the civil rights issue would return to haunt the Kennedy administration.

Putting a man into space in May 1961, albeit a month after the Russians, gave the country a boost. Jack appreciated the prestige of being ahead in the space race and spoke of the United States putting a man on the moon before the end of the decade. Jack's first year in office ended with another family tragedy, when 73-year-old Joe had a massive stroke, leaving him partly paralyzed and without speech. Joe had orchestrated his son's rise to the White House, but the President could no longer look to him for advice and support. On the other hand, he no longer had to worry about living up to Joe's expectations or seeking his approval. And even before his father became incapacitated, Jack had begun asserting his independence. The discussions between them had become increasingly perfunctory. No one could now accuse Jack of not being his own man.

Head of Ford Motor Co. gets defense portfolio

Opposite above: The President confers with his new Defense Secretary, Robert McNamara. McNamara was a typical "New Frontiersman" in the Kennedy administration. A year older than Jack, he was an intellectual but with a reputation for getting things done. Jack lured him from his post as head of the Ford Motor Co., and was not unduly worried about his Republican leanings.

Opposite below: Kennedy liked to take soundings from liberal intellectuals, such as Harvard professor Arthur Schlesinger Jr., who was appointed as a special adviser. However, he was a pragmatist by instinct, and was more interested in achieving immediate goals than in long-term strategic planning.

Above: The President-elect braves the elements as he leaves for yet another function held in his honor. The Inauguration also took place in freezing conditions, yet Jack made a point of appearing hatless and without an overcoat. He liked to present an image of athleticism and vigor, but on that occasion he made sure he was wearing thermal underwear.

Inagaural day

Opposite: The presidential party is given an enthusiastic reception during the Inaugural parade. Green dye had been sprayed on the grass to give an appearance of spring instead of winter, and flamethrowers were used to melt the snow that fell in the hours leading up to the ceremony.

Above: The outgoing chief executive Dwight Eisenhower was 70 when he left office, making him the then oldest man to occupy the White House. At 43, JFK was the youngest elected president ever. Eisenhower told his successor that the situation in Southeast Asia would give him much cause for concern. Despite their differences, Kennedy subscribed to Eisenhower's view that the countries of Indochina could fall to Communism one by one at an alarming rate, a world view that came to be known as the Domino Theory.

Right: The Kennedys leave the Capitol building at the end of the ceremony, which saw Jack sworn in as the 35th President of United States. Jackie was extremely ill on the day, and the Kennedys' personal physician Janet Travell prescribed Dexedrine to help her get through the exhausting schedule.

Accompanied by Sinatra

Above: Frank Sinatra escorts Jackie to her box for a glittering evening of entertainment at the National Guard Armory on the eve of the Inauguration. Jack gave Sinatra a warm vote of thanks for organizing the fund-raiser. Sinatra saw the tribute as recognition of the part he had played in getting Kennedy elected. Jackie's white satin gown was designed by Oleg Cassini.

Gala celebrations

Above: The presidential box at the Inaugural Ball. Joe and Rose Kennedy are seated to the President's right. Jackie is in conversation with Lyndon Johnson, and Teddy and Joan Kennedy sit behind. Gala celebrations were held at five different venues to usher in the new administration. Jackie cut her evening short and returned to the White House alone. Jack partied long into the night.

Right: The Kennedys return to Washington after a weekend break in Palm Beach. Jack had just made his first State of the Union address, in which he warned of the dangers posed by Communism. Caroline and John Jr. had to remain in Palm Beach initially, while Jackie supervised getting their rooms at the White House ready. The press was out in force on February 4, when Jack and Jackie finally brought the children home. Jackie swaddled John Jr. in blankets, trying to shield the baby from his first taste of media intrusion.

First Bill signed
and Peace Corps founded

Above: Congressmen from both Houses present Jack with a pair of cuff links to mark the signing of his first Bill as chief executive, which increased the amount of government food surpluses to be distributed to the country's poorest families.

Left: Kennedy deflects media questions regarding the "missile gap" between the United States and the Soviet Union. There was indeed a gap—in America's favor. During the election campaign, Jack preserved the fiction of superior Soviet arms capability for political purposes.

Opposite above: Bobby Kennedy's wife, Ethel (left), attends a press conference with Jean and Eunice Kennedy. The theme was the Peace Corps, one of Jack's most popular and successful initiatives. The idea was to send highly skilled volunteers to developing countries, where they would give assistance in any number of areas, from infrastructure projects to social policy matters. The conference was led by Sargent Shriver, Eunice Kennedy's husband, who was charged with implementing the program.

Opposite below: March 1, 1960. Kennedy invites Eleanor Roosevelt to the White House on the day the Peace Corps officially comes into being. The President was always eager to exploit the public relations value of any policy announcements.

Alliance for Progress

Opposite above: The last Democratic president, Harry S. Truman, pays a visit to the Oval Office. Unlike his father, Jack had been a supporter of the Truman Doctrine, which gave aid to European countries to help stave off the threat of Communism. It was not a mutual appreciation society, however. Truman had grave reservations about Kennedy's suitability for the role of chief executive.

Opposite below: Kennedy visits Honduras, where he is received by President Ramón Villeda. Jack had talks with leaders of all Central American countries during his visit, apprising them of his Alliance for Progress initiative. Its aim was to help improve the economies and welfare systems of Latin American countries. This was not implemented purely for altruistic reasons. Kennedy knew that grinding poverty and lack of access to decent housing, education, and health care would inevitably mean continuing political instability. It was not in the United States' interest to see the rise to power of more revolutionaries like Fidel Castro, the Cuban leader who had overthrown the Batista government in 1959.

Above: Caroline Kennedy plays with her two-month-old baby brother.

President warns of threat to Laos

Left: March 22, 1961. Kennedy uses a map of Southeast Asia to illustrate the growth of Communism in the region. He highlighted the strategic importance of preventing Laos from becoming the next domino to fall. However, the Bay of Pigs reversal made Jack think twice about a military option, which some of his advisers were already recommending. Instead, Jack favored a continuation of aid in support of those fighting the Communist Pathet Lao, who were being backed by North Vietnam and the Soviet Union. If a pro-Western regime could not take control in Laos, Jack felt that the second-best option was to secure a cease-fire and neutrality for the country. This would be high on the agenda during Kennedy's summit meeting with Khrushchev in June.

First Lady plans grand White House refurbishment scheme

Left: The First Lady, pictured after attending an Easter service at Palm Beach. Almost as soon as she took up residence at the White House, Jackie instituted plans for a grand refurbishment program. She had been dismayed by the contents when her predecessor, Mamie Eisenhower, invited her to take a tour of the mansion. Her plan was to remove all the bad reproductions and restore the White House in a grand style befitting its traditions. Due to the restricted funds available for the project, she arranged to borrow paintings from the National Gallery and Smithsonian. She also asked around among friends to see if they could contribute suitable trinkets and ornaments.

Below: In early March, Jackie's sister, Lee, came to stay at the White House with her second husband, Stanislaus Radziwill. Radziwill was a Polish prince who became a successful property developer in Britain after leaving his homeland during the war. Jackie went to great lengths to impress her sister and brother-in-law, treating them more like foreign dignitaries than family. Jackie accompanied the Radziwills to Glen Ora, the Kennedy's newly acquired country retreat, and they then went on to New York, where Jackie indulged her passion for antiques hunting.

Take me out to the ball game

Above: Jack and his sister Jean, pictured at a baseball game in April 1961. Team sports continued to play a big part in the family's lives. Jackie had little time for such diversions. Just three months had elapsed since the Kennedys had taken up residence at the White House, yet Jackie was already spending a considerable amount of time away from Washington. She decided she had little choice but to give Jack the space and freedom to relax with his coterie of male friends. Various parts of the White House were used for holding parties in her absence, from the swimming

The United States will forge ahead in space race

Above: At work in the Oval Office. Kennedy allowed journalists unprecedented access to the center of power as an exercise in open government, and to build his approval ratings. In an early speech, he had pledged to make inroads into the lead the Soviet Union enjoyed in the field of space technology. A month after Yuri Gagarin orbited the earth, Alan Shepard became the United States' first astronaut. After Shepard's 15-minute flight had taken him 115 miles into space, Kennedy declared the country's aim to put a man on the moon before the end of the decade.

Opposite above: A good-humored moment shared by Kennedy and the British Prime Minister Harold Macmillan. The two leaders met for the first time in Washington in early April and got on well.

Opposite below: Jack and former president Eisenhower tour the grounds of Camp David.

Camp David

Left: Jack canvasses the opinion of Eisenhower, in the wake of the Bay of Pigs debacle. The plan to invade Cuba using a brigade of exiles from the country was hatched by the CIA during the Eisenhower administration. When Jack took office, the head of the CIA, Allen Dulles, and his deputy, Richard Bissell, sought permission to carry the plan through. Jack was circumspect, but gave his guarded approval because there was near unanimous agreement that there would be a successful outcome. It turned into a catalog of error and misjudgment, which bordered on the farcical. Publicly, Jack took full responsibility; in private, he was livid with the advisers who he felt had misled him. As a distinguished military man, Eisenhower was scathing about the way the operation was handled.

Overcoming her nerves

Above: Jack and Jackie relax at Palm Beach ahead of a heavy touring schedule. It began with a state visit to Canada on May 17. This was followed by a trip to Paris and Vienna, where the Kennedys would meet political heavyweights Charles de Gaulle and Nikita Khrushchev. Jackie was still riddled with self-doubt over the role of First Lady, particularly when she had to play hostess to a steady stream of senior diplomats and heads of state. The conflict between her distaste for the role and her desire to discharge her duties took a heavy emotional toll. She had mood swings, headaches, and depression. Ironically, however, it was during the visit to Canada and Europe that she grabbed the headlines, beguiled some of the world's foremost statesmen, and established herself as a star performer on the international stage.

Opposite above: Jack enjoying a round of golf at Palm Beach with his father and brothers-in-law, Stephen Smith (left) and Peter Lawford.

Opposite below: April 1961. Kennedy receives Indonesia's President Sukarno at Andrews Air Force Base. He quickly concluded that international affairs was the field that mattered most and the one in which he would make his mark as a statesman.

44th birthday celebrations

Left: May 29, 1961. Kennedy is guest of honor at Boston's Commonwealth Armory as he celebrates his 44th birthday. With him is Cardinal Richard Cushing, a long-standing family friend who had officiated at many Kennedy weddings, baptisms, and funerals. After Kennedy's assassination, the Cardinal admitted being party to distributing donations to various ministries during the election campaign. The link between moneys paid and votes accrued was clearly established.

Above: Jack making an address to Congress at the State of the Union address, May 25, 1961.

Opposite: Commitment to the space race inevitably meant huge financial investment. Jack goes before Congress to ask for between 7 and 9 billion dollars over a five-year period. The request was approved, allowing the *Apollo* program to get underway.

The toast of Paris

Above: Leaving the Elysée Palace, where the Kennedys had dined with President De Gaulle. Both made a favorable impression on the French leader, although he thought the President's youth was a handicap. After the bitter experience the French had in Indochina, he warned Kennedy of the dangers of becoming embroiled in a conflict in that region.

Opposite above: Jackie's glamour and style, together with her appreciation of the French language and culture, win over the Parisian crowds. She is depicted leaving the Jeu de Paume gallery, famous for its Impressionist paintings.

Opposite below: Kennedy, pictured with some of his top aides. They were summoned to France to prepare the strategic line Jack would take in the summit with Soviet leader Nikita Khrushchev. The guidance and advice received could hardly have prepared him for the encounter. Khrushchev easily got the better of him when the two engaged in a debate on political philosophy. At every turn of the discussion Kennedy found the Soviet leader aggressive and intransigent. When the summit was over, Jack likened negotiating with Khrushchev to dealing with his father; in both cases it was he who was expected to defer.

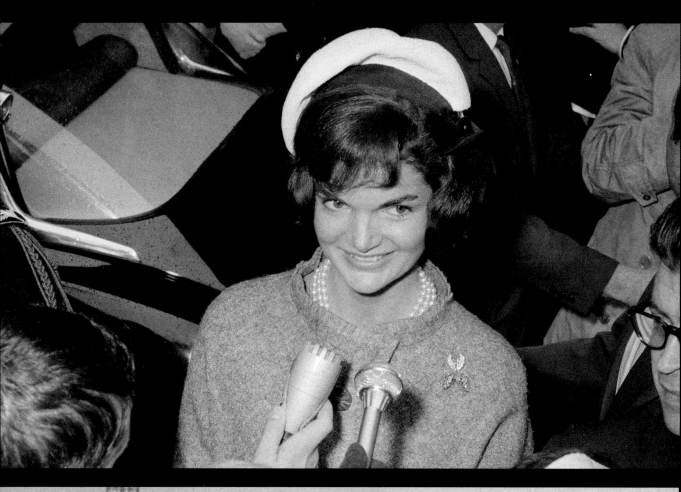

President and First Lady at Buckingham Palace

Above: The Kennedys ended their state visit to Europe in London. After attending the christening of Prince and Princess Radziwill's daughter, Christina, the President and First Lady were guests of honor at a banquet hosted by Queen Elizabeth II at Buckingham Palace. It was the first time a U.S. president had dined at the Palace since 1918, when Woodrow Wilson visited King George V. For Jack, the most important part of this final leg of the trip was to seek Macmillan's advice on his uncomfortable experience at the Vienna summit.

Opposite above: Vienna, June 3, 1961. The official photocall for the leaders of the East and West suggested a cordial relationship. In fact, Kennedy came away from the two-day summit somewhat shell shocked. Khrushchev was militaristic, threatening to sign a treaty with East Germany that would put the security of West Berlin at risk.

Opposite below: Khrushchev was much more taken with the First Lady than with the President. After outmaneuvering Kennedy during their first meeting, the Soviet leader repeated the trick at the evening's state dinner, held at Schönbrunn Palace. Reporters wanted the leaders to shake hands; Khruschev joked that he preferred to shake Jackie's hand first.

The war on crime

Above: September 13, 1961. The President signs the Crime Bill, with both the Attorney General, Robert Kennedy, and FBI Director J. Edgar Hoover (second left) in attendance. Mafia bosses were said to be angry at the administration's war against organized crime. They regarded this as a betrayal of the preelection understanding, which had seen them working behind the scenes for a Democratic victory.

Opposite: After a successful six-month trial period, the Peace Corps becomes enshrined in law. Kennedy shakes hands with his brother-in-law Sargent Shriver, the organization's first director.

Action man—with a little help from Dr. Feel Good

Above: Jack arriving at Andrews Air Force Base en route to Hyannis Port, early November 1961. The picture suggests vitality, but Jack had been experiencing considerable back pain in recent months and had been taking a cocktail of medicines to ease the condition. The man who administered them was Max Jacobson, a New York physician with a cult following who was known as Dr. Feel Good. Jackie also received regular injections from Jacobson.

Opposite above: Jack temporarily puts aside the affairs of state to enjoy a cigar at a Washington banquet in late September 1961. Privately, he was highly critical of his own performance during his first nine months in office.

Opposite below: Former head of the CIA, Allen Dulles, receives a National Security Award from the President. Dulles resigned in the wake of the Bay of Pigs fiasco. Jack took the flak in public, but in private he was scathing about the contribution of some of his senior advisers, including Dulles.

A first interview with *Izvestia*

Opposite above: November 25, 1961. Jack discusses U.S. nuclear policy with Aleksei Adzhubei, the editor of *Izvestia* and also Nikita Khrushchev's son-in-law. It was the first time the Soviet Union's official newspaper had carried an interview with a U.S. president.

Opposite below: December 1961. Jackie dazzles the Venezuelan public with a speech in La Morita, delivered in perfect Spanish. Looking on is the country's president, Rómulo Betancourt. He and Colombia's Alberto Camargo were two of Latin America's most progressive leaders, and Jack deliberately chose these two countries for his first presidential visit to this region. In supporting these regimes, Jack believed it would be more difficult for Communism to make significant inroads.

Right: Jackie's first official photograph as the wife of the President. This portrait, by New York photographer Mark Shaw, was used to satisfy the huge number of requests for a picture of the First Lady.

Below: Jack and Jackie attend church service at Palm Beach, December 24, 1961. The seasonal family celebrations were overshadowed by the severe stroke that Joe Kennedy suffered on December 19.

CHAPTER FIVE

Crisis and Separation 1962

The new year brought a host of new crises: domestic, foreign, and personal. It started well enough. On February 20, John Glenn became the first American to orbit the earth, vindicating the vocal and financial support Kennedy had pledged to the space program. This achievement came hard on the heels of a political coup: the release of Gary Powers. Powers had been held in Russia on spying charges since May 1960, when his U-2 plane had been shot down. The quid pro quo for Powers' release had been freeing Colonel Rudolph Abel, who was himself serving a 30-year jail sentence as a Russian spy.

Jack had barely had time to bask in the glory of these achievements when he was embroiled in a confrontation with the steel industry. He was furious when some of the country's top industrialists raised their prices when he had specifically called for restraint from both sides of industry. Fearing the loss of lucrative government contracts and legal action under antimonopoly laws, the will of the steel men slowly crumbled. Kennedy also made it clear that they risked having any dirt in their private lives exposed. With a combination of carrot and stick, he got his way.

Predictably, Republicans were incandescent, regarding the President's intervention as an unwarranted attack on the free enterprise culture, which was central to the country's values. Jack saw the need to redress the balance. Having made his point, during the remainder of his tenure he instituted a string of measures that helped big business, and in summer 1962 he agreed to a $10 billion tax cut, which went into the pockets of the country's wealthiest people.

Meanwhile, the cracks continued to show in the Kennedys' marriage. Jack didn't let the affairs of state get in the way of his womanizing. There were many casual conquests, and he initiated a more intense liaison with Mary Meyer, a woman he knew from his college days. Meyer, Judith Campbell, and any number of others represented a potential threat to the presidency, but at least they were relatively anonymous figures. The same could hardly be said of Marilyn Monroe. Exactly when Jack first met the screen legend is unclear, but the reverberations of their relationship would soon be echoing through the White House. Jack's weakness for beautiful women and Hollywood glitz, together with Monroe's drink- and drug-fueled instability, would prove to be a dangerous cocktail.

To mark the refurbishment of the presidential home, Jackie hosted a network television program in which she described the renovations and acquisitions that had been made. Jack had been apprehensive about how the alterations would play with the public. He didn't need to worry as the program was greeted with enthusiasm. The following month, Jackie embarked on a solo three-week trip to India and Pakistan. She charmed the respective heads of state, Nehru and Ayub Khan, no mean diplomatic feat given the political sensitivies in that part of the world. Jackie would take many more single trips thereafter, physical separation reflecting the emotional distance between them.

The Kennedys spent Easter at Palm Beach, where Joe was preparing for a lengthy rehabilitation program. Jack returned to Washington at the end of April for talks with Macmillan. Britain's premier was not being accompanied by his wife, Lady Dorothy, so Jackie stayed on at Palm Beach.

Opposite: JFK poses in his rocking chair.

The two leaders met just as the United States resumed atmospheric nuclear tests at Christmas Island. Macmillan was unhappy that Kennedy had sanctioned this response to the Soviet testing program without first consulting him.

On May 19, a gala evening was held at Madison Square Garden to mark Jack's forthcoming 45th birthday. Marilyn Monroe stole the show with her gossamer outfit and breathy rendition of "Happy Birthday." Jackie, perhaps fearing that she risked having her nose rubbed in her husband's tawdry affairs, had chosen to attend a horse show in Virginia instead.

Monroe besieged Jack with calls over the following weeks. Bobby's involvement with the star complicated matters further, and by late June Jack was anxious to sever all relations between her and the Kennedy family.

On Saturday, August 4, Monroe telephoned Jack's brother-in-law, Peter Lawford, informing him that she had taken a lot of pills. She died the following day. After a hasty investigation, the police returned a verdict of "probable suicide." Speculation about the exact sequence of events has continued ever since. Bobby is said to have had a stormy encounter with Monroe the day before her death. The other questions surround a possible clean-up operation, in which all material linking Monroe with the Kennedys was removed before the police arrived on the scene, and the speed of the investigation prompted suggestions that the police had been pressured from above.

The summer of 1962 also saw a series of events that brought the world to the brink of nuclear conflagration. It began in July, when Khrushchev agreed to a request from Castro for military aid. The Soviet leader was sympathetic to Castro's concerns that the United States might be planning to invade Cuba. He was also intent on getting the upper hand on a president he believed he could dominate. Both Khrushchev and Kennedy knew that the "missile gap," which Jack had warned of during his election campaign, was a complete fiction: it was the United States that held the military advantage in all departments. Khrushchev knew that placing nuclear warheads on Cuban soil would more than compensate for the overall superiority that the United States enjoyed.

Soviet Foreign Minister Andrei Gromyko repeatedly maintained that the weapons buildup was purely a defensive capability. Jack initially gave the Soviet leadership the benefit of the doubt, much to the chagrin of hawkish right wingers at home. On October 15, a U-2 reconnaissance plane flew over the island and revealed the existence of missile sites with an offensive capability. Jack set up the executive committee of the National Security Council to consider what action the United States should take. Over the next two weeks, Excomm, whose number included Bobby, Dean Rusk, and Robert McNamara, was in session virtually around the clock.

Once the idea of a full-scale invasion of Cuba had been dismissed, two options were on the table: a surgical strike and a blockade. Neither was particularly palatable. The success of a targeted strike could not be guaranteed and would almost certainly lead to an escalation. A blockade would be difficult to enforce and wouldn't address the problem of the forces and the hardware already present on the island. It was also dubious in terms of international law.

Jack finally came down in favor of the latter option, neatly sidestepping the legal issue by calling the proposed response a "quarantine line" instead of a blockade.

On October 22, he broadcast to the nation, condemning the Soviet Union's provocative action and making it clear that the United States' resolve was unshakable. Despite the gravity of the situation, there were a few dissenting voices as the country swung behind its leader. There was also United Nations support, following representations to the Security Council by the American ambassador Adlai Stevenson. Stevenson gave a masterly performance, teasing out denial after denial from the Soviet delegates before dramatically revealing the damning evidence. However, the confrontation was to be staged not in a debating chamber, but on the high seas.

On October 4, two Soviet ships and a submarine approached the quarantine zone. Jack had drawn the line; now he could only wait to see if Khrushchev would cross it. Tensions temporarily eased when the vessels were reported to have turned back. This small victory prompted Rusk's celebrated remark that the enemy had "blinked first."

Above: Jackie, pictured during her successful solo trip to India and Pakistan in the spring of 1962.

Jack realized that Khrushchev would not countenance total humiliating defeat. A face-saving compromise was needed. A Soviet withdrawal from Cuba in exchange for a guarantee that the United States would not invade the island seemed to have done the trick. But in a subsequent communication from Moscow, Khrushchev added a rider

that Jupiter missiles had to be removed from Turkish soil. Kennedy took a calculated gamble. He insisted that the first message should form the basis of the settlement to the immediate crisis, but let it be known that the issue of missiles in Turkey would be addressed in due course. Khrushchev accepted, leaving Castro fuming. In April the following year, when the dust had settled, Jupiter missiles were indeed withdrawn from Turkey.

Jack was applauded for his statesmanship and for keeping a cool head in such a crisis. His approval rating went through the roof, reflected in the strong Democrat showing in the midterm Congressional elections. Others said he'd been very lucky. The plan of action had been uncertain at times, and Kennedy had boxed himself in by imposing the quarantine.

On the domestic front, the burning issue was still civil rights. Despite the unrest of the previous year, Jack still showed great reluctance to act. The celebrated "stroke of the pen" was finally delivered in November 1962. The White House had been deluged with pens in the post, a reproachful reminder of the famous election pledge. Civil rights leaders felt that Kennedy had been dragged kicking and screaming to deliver the order instead of rushing to sign of his own volition. Jack, of course, had one eye on Southern congressmen, whom he had no wish to antagonize.

He had not anguished over the civil rights question in his formative years. This was not out of callous disregard for the plight of those less fortunate; the issue simply didn't touch the privileged life of the young Bostonian. After taking office, things should have been different. However, the mature Kennedy was also a hard-nosed politician, and he knew that any action on civil rights was bound to invite praise and vitriol in equal measure.

The perceived tepid action at the top contrasted sharply with white-hot emotions on the ground. They boiled over in September 1962, when James Meredith attempted to enroll at the all-white University of Mississippi. State Governor Ross Barnett intervened on the side of the segregationists. He was determined to defy all moves, including a Supreme Court order, to allow Meredith entry to the university. He finally yielded, but as federal marshals escorted Meredith onto the campus, a riot broke out and there were two fatalities. Kennedy emerged with little credit. In their venomous chants the white mob made clear their disgust at White House involvement in the Meredith case. Nor did he impress the likes of Martin Luther King Jr., who felt Kennedy had failed to give a strong moral lead on the issue.

At the end of 1962, however, most Americans focused on Kennedy's handling of the Cuban crisis in assessing the President's second year in office. That Christmas also saw the release of more than a thousand prisoners captured during the Bay of Pigs incident. His stock rose even higher as he met the grateful brigade members at the Miami Orange Bowl. The narrow margin of the election victory over Nixon was now a distant memory. Kennedy gave an upbeat assessment of the previous 12 months, focusing on the country's role in preventing the spread of Communism. Politically, he now looked untouchable. Privately, he may have been less enamored with the responsibilities of office. When the Cuban crisis hung perilously in the balance, an exhausted Kennedy had remarked: "If they want this job they can have it. It's no great joy to me."

Opposite: Jack and Jackie at a function in November 1962. As their second year in the White House drew to a close, both enjoyed enormous popularity.

Left: Leaving mass at Hyannis Port.

Glenn orbits the earth

Left: The beginning of Kennedy's second year in office brought a mixed bag of news. On February 13, the President announced that the release of U-2 pilot Gary Powers had been negotiated. Powers had been held by the Soviet Union since May 1960, when his plane was shot down over Soviet airspace. A week later, John Glenn became the first American astronaut to orbit the earth. However, there were difficulties ahead. The first American serviceman had been killed in Southeast Asia, and before the year was out, civil rights and Cuba would return to haunt the administration.

Jackie's year of escape

Above: Jackie attends a Democratic Party function to mark her husband's first anniversary as president. This was to be a rare sight in 1962. Having enchanted a host of world leaders the previous year, Jackie would build on those achievements in the following 12 months. This time, however, she would do so without her husband in attendance. There were extended vacations as well as political trips, which meant that the couple spent a considerable amount of time apart.

State of the Union

Left: JFK delivers his second State of the Union address. It outlined 34 legislative measures, including increased federal spending on education and medical care for the elderly. He would get fewer than half of his proposals through Congress. Committees packed with Republicans and Southern Democrats would be a constant thorn in his side, particularly in areas of liberal reform.

Below: The President and First Lady welcome the composer Igor Stravinsky to the White House. Occasions such as this reaffirmed Kennedy's stated aim to associate the center of government with high culture. The link between artistic and political freedoms became a recurring theme.

Papal audience

Above: March 10, 1962. Before her trip to meet the Indian and Pakistani heads of state, Jackie stops off at the Vatican. Her audience with Pope John XXIII was also partly diplomatic in nature. Jackie pleaded the case of her sister, Lee, who was seeking an annulment of her first marriage, to Michael Canfield. The Church did not recognize their divorce, or Lee's subsequent marriage to Stanislaus Radziwill, which took place in a civil ceremony in 1958. Jackie's intercession had the desired effect, the Vatican agreeing to the annulment in November that year.

Kennedy takes on steel industry

Right: March 1962. Jack receives an honorary degree from the University of California, Berkeley. He was embroiled in a major confrontation with the steel industry at the time. The magnates who ran the corporations eventually buckled under government pressure, rescinding inflationary price rises that Kennedy had described as unjustified. Relationships between the White House and the business community were uneasy thereafter, particularly after Kennedy remarked: "My father always told me that all businessmen were sons of bitches but I never believed it till now."

Above: Rose Kennedy has a quiet word with her son during the Joseph P. Kennedy Jr. Foundation dinner. Rose met her husband's incapacity with fortitude. Eventually, she delegated the role of primary carer to a niece, Ann Gargan. Joe's condition meant that Jackie had lost her main ally in the family.

The United States resumes nuclear testing

Right: While Jackie was courting Nehru and Ayub, the premiers of India and Pakistan, Jack had much to occupy him at home. Against his wishes, he felt compelled to authorize the resumption of nuclear testing, the Soviet Union having done so the previous year. This was to be a precursor to a potentially cataclysmic confrontation between the superpowers over Cuba. The civil rights issue was also about to boil over again. Black leaders were still waiting for "the stroke of the pen" with which Kennedy had promised to end discrimination. Away from the affairs of state, Jack was as adventurous as ever. His father's stroke had, if anything, made him even more determined to live for the moment. He duly plunged into an affair with an old college friend, Mary Meyer, which reached new heights of intensity and recklessness.

Diplomatic coup for Jackie

Above: Jackie and her sister enjoy a leisurely form of transportation, Indian style. The First Lady had made a great impression on Jawaharlal Nehru during his visit to Washington the previous fall. Jack had found Nehru difficult, and relations between the two were not helped by India's recent invasion of Goa, a Portuguese colony on the country's west coast. That, together with the fact that the next port of call was Pakistan, made this no easy baptism for Jackie in her first solo performance on the diplomatic stage. She carried it off with aplomb.

Opposite: Jackie and Lee, pictured at the Radziwills' home in London after completing the successful visit to India. Lee effectively acted as Jackie's lady-in-waiting during the trip, and although she executed those duties diligently, she was jealous of the star status accorded her older sister. There was a competitiveness between them, which mirrored that between the Kennedy siblings.

Right: Jackie leaves Lee's house in Buckingham Place to attend a dinner at Buckingham Palace, the last official function of her three-week trip. The sisters' relationship survived the fact that Lee was said to be another of Jack's conquests.

Hoover applies pressure

Above: Jack was full of praise for Jackie's diplomatic triumph in India and Pakistan and welcomed her home with a lavish reception. He was also extremely indulgent when Jackie asked him to make arrangements for the importation of a magnificent horse presented to her by Pakistan's president Ayub Khan. Even as he was displaying such open affection, Jack was maneuvering to protect himself from J. Edgar Hoover. On March 22, a week before Jackie's return, the FBI chief informed the President that he was aware of the affair between him and Judith Campbell, and that Campbell was also the mistress of Mafia boss Sam Giancana. This was not the only piece of salacious information Hoover had on Kennedy, which was undoubtedly the reason Jack kept him on when he took office. He had no wish to make an enemy of Hoover, and quickly severed all ties with Campbell.

Left: Jack was fond of gadgets, particularly telecommunications technology. In the Oval Office he had an 18-button telephone installed, through which he conducted a lot of presidential business. He is pictured sending a signal from Palm Beach via satellite to officially open the 1962 World's Fair in Seattle.

"Happy Birthday Mr. President"

Above: Jack pitches the first ball of the 1962 baseball season, following a presidential tradition dating back to the time of William Taft.

On May 19, Jack attended a Democratic Party function at Madison Square Garden, which was both a fund-raiser and an advanced celebration of his 45th birthday. It was at this event that Marilyn Monroe, attired in a gossamer, skintight gown, appeared on stage to sing "Happy Birthday." The performance was so sultry and provocative that journalist Dorothy Kilgallen likened it to "making love to the President in direct view of 40 million Americans."

Jack had first met Monroe in November 1961. Given his weakness for beautiful women and Hollywood glamour, the affair was hardly surprising. Monroe invested more in the relationship than Jack did, even entertaining hopes that he might leave Jackie and marry her. Jackie was spared her overtly sexual Madison Square Garden performance, choosing instead to attend a Virginia horse show with Caroline.

Ransom agreed for Bay of Pigs hostages

Above: Enjoying a family break at Palm Springs, Easter 1962. Jack was engaged in behind-the-scenes negotiations to secure the release of those captured during the Bay of Pigs invasion. At first he was determined not to yield to Castro's huge ransom demands, because it would have been at odds with the high standards of integrity he had said would characterize his administration. Ultimately, however, he agreed to pay $56 million in cash and goods to secure the release of more than a thousand prisoners.

Left: Jackie shows off John Jr. to the Empress of Iran during a state visit, April 1962.

Opposite: April 28, 1962. The Kennedys return to Washington to prepare for the visit of Harold Macmillan. Relations between Kennedy and Macmillan remained good, although they disagreed over nuclear testing. Macmillan urged Kennedy to show restraint in the hope of securing a test-ban agreement with the Soviet Union. Jack authorized the resumption of testing without consulting Macmillan, incurring the latter's anger. Even so, many of Kennedy's senior advisers were concerned that he was being unduly influenced by his British counterpart.

Concerns over Soviet arms in Cuba

Left: May 4, 1962. Jack, surrounded by some of the top brass during a military display at Eglin Air Base, Florida. American forces would soon be on a war footing. The early months of 1962 had seen a steady stream of Soviet military personnel and weaponry flow into Cuba. Jack and his advisers kept the situation under review, and were prepared to tolerate the buildup, provided it was only a defensive capability. The First Lady continued to spend much of her time away from her husband. In early May, she paid a surprise visit to her father-in-law, who was attempting his first steps since having a stroke six months earlier.

Political power and high culture

Opposite: The worsening situation in Laos was the theme of this news conference, held on May 9, 1962. Kennedy announced that Communist forces were continuing to make inroads into the country, a clear breach of the cease-fire agreement. Two months later, in July 1962, both the United States and the Soviet Union endorsed the Geneva Accords, which established a neutralist government under Prince Souvanna Phouma. Under its terms, all external factions were to withdraw. In fact, the war merely became a covert operation. Hanoi continued its support of the Communist Pathet Lao, while the United States initiated a counter-insurgency program. With Kennedy's approval, the CIA recruited thousands of Laotian tribesmen who acted as guerrilla warriors.

Left: In formal attire for one of the many gala dinners that the President and First Lady held at the White House. Jackie was the driving force behind such occasions, and the guest list included Tennessee Williams, Arthur Miller, Pablo Casals, Leonard Bernstein, and Mark Rothko. Jack's cultural interests were somewhat more lowbrow, and he occasionally had to be prompted on which field the visitors excelled in. On one such occasion, a dinner given in honor of a host of Nobel Prize winners, Jack remarked: "I think that this is the most extraordinary collection of human knowledge that has ever been gathered together at the White House—with the possible exception of when Thomas Jefferson dined alone."

Below: The Kennedys on the front lawn of the White House.

The Oval Office as playground

Left: The Oval Office was not off limits to the Kennedy children. Jack encouraged them to come and play in the room that was the seat of power. Here, in May 1962, he delights in seeing John Jr. take some of his first faltering steps. Jack is sitting on the desk Jackie rescued from an unused room when they took up residence at the White House. Made from the timbers of HMS *Resolute*, it was presented to President Rutherford Hayes by Queen Victoria in 1878. The naval theme was continued with several artifacts, including the coconut shell on which Jack wrote his famous SOS message during the survival ordeal of 1943.

United front

Left: Jack and Jackie show a united front as they receive delegates to a Democratic Women's conference at the White House. It was shortly after Marilyn Monroe's show-stopping performance, and the actress was now bombarding the White House with calls day and night. Jackie herself is said to have received one of these impassioned messages. As was her custom, the First Lady met the inevitable gossip and speculation with serene dignity.

Below: The President and First Lady greet the American Ballet Company before they give a performance at the White House. Jackie was at her husband's side at a number of engagements in the week following Monroe's Madison Square Garden performance. At one banquet she wore a gown not dissimilar to the one in which Monroe had caused such a sensation. Jackie had recently hosted a dinner at which playwright Arthur Miller was an honored guest. Miller, one of the victims of the McCarthy witch hunts, had just remarried after divorcing Monroe.

Jackie's restoration triumph

Right: Jackie shows off the newly restored Treaty Room, which had served as the Cabinet Room during Lincoln's presidency. At the end of her grand restoration of the White House, she hosted a television program in which she described the improvements and acquisitions. Ever mindful of the public relations angle, Jack was apprehensive about the venture, but Jackie carried it off impressively.

Below: The Kennedys received a rapturous welcome in Mexico City. Jackie won everybody over with her beauty and elegance, not to mention an address delivered in perfect Spanish. However, a month beforehand Jack had brazenly invited Mary Meyer to a White House dinner, which—coming on top of the Monroe affair—had made Jackie seek the sanctuary of Glen Ora; she had only returned to Washington shortly before the official visit to Mexico.

Increasing pressure

Opposite: After a nine-month-long White House social season peppered with cultural events, watching a baseball game comes as something of a relief. The summer months brought increasing concerns over the buildup of Soviet forces in Cuba, although Jack remained unconvinced that this constituted a threat. He focused a lot of attention on the midterm Congressional election campaign, frustrated that so many legislative measures were being blocked. At the time he was experimenting with various medicines to combat his medical problems—in addition to Novocain and cortisone, he was introduced to amphetamines by Max Jacobson, the guru to the rich and famous known as Dr. Feel Good. After months of supporting the President in her official capacity—and helping boost his popularity—Jackie sought sanctuary away from the limelight. In August, she took Caroline to Ravello, Italy, where the Radziwills had rented a villa. Mary Meyer was a regular visitor to the White House in her absence.

First Lady's vacation irks President—and voters

Left: Ravello offered no escape from the world's press, who were out in force to get a shot of the First Lady. Pictures of her in a bathing suit raised eyebrows at home because some Americans felt it was undignified for a woman in her position. The coverage got even worse for Jackie when she was reported to be spending a lot of time in the company of Gianni Agnelli, one of the jet-setters who was in the party. Jack was more annoyed with the political fallout than the suggestion of any impropriety. He cabled Jackie the terse instruction: "Less Agnelli, more Caroline."

Opposite: Jack at work in the Oval Office, late August 1962. He was irked by Jackie's decision to extend her vacation in Italy. Many American voters were, too, particularly women's groups who felt she was abdicating her responsibilities by cavorting abroad when her place was at home supporting the President. Jack responded by insisting that Jackie and Caroline return home before the end of the month. She took him at his word, arriving at Newport on August 31.

Below: Jack visits Cape Canaveral, where he meets the first American to orbit the earth, Colonel John Glenn. Kennedy had awarded Glenn the Distinguished Service Medal for the historic flight on *Friendship 7* in February 1962. Hovering in the background is Vice President Lyndon Johnson. Johnson hated the role, in which he felt emasculated. Having relinquished the power base he enjoyed as Senate leader, he had little executive authority in the Kennedy administration. Diplomatic visits overseas would be the highlights of his tenure in the number two job.

"The new frontier of science and space"

Above: September 12, 1962. In a speech at Rice University, Texas, Jack reaffirms his vision for the United States to lead the world in space technology, and the objective of reaching the moon before the end of the decade. Houston would be at the center of this technological revolution: "What was once the farthest outpost on the old frontier of the West will be the farthest outpost on the new frontier of science and space."

Opposite: Newport, Rhode Island, September 14, 1962. Jackie, at a dinner to mark the finals of the America's Cup. She and the children spent most of the month at Hammersmith Farm. On September 12, Jack flew from Washington to join her as they celebrated their ninth wedding anniversary. On top of the negative press reports concerning Jackie's vacation, rumors began to circulate that in 1947 Jack had been briefly married to a woman named Durie Malcolm.

Left: Jackie, accompanied by John D. Rockefeller III at the opening of the Philharmonic Hall at the Lincoln Center.

Riots as black student enrols in Mississippi

Left: September 30, 1962. The President delivers a broadcast to try to defuse the volatile situation surrounding James Meredith's enrolment at the University of Mississippi. Meredith, a 29-year-old black ex-serviceman, had been inspired by Kennedy's inaugural address and applied to enter his home state's university. When he was rejected, he took his case to court, eventually winning on appeal. Mississippi's governor, Ross Barnett, expressed his intention to defy the ruling. An internecine domestic conflict was the last thing Jack wanted at such a time, but he gave the order for federal troops to be deployed. He broadcast to the nation as Meredith was being escorted onto the campus. Two speeches were prepared, depending on whether the enrolment had been carried out peacefully or not. Even as he began reading the speech suggesting the situation in Mississippi was calm, violence erupted. There were many casualties and two fatalities. Kennedy was applauded for what was seen as his determination to uphold one individual's rights. Black leaders were less impressed, feeling that Kennedy was still dragging his heels on civil rights legislation.

Bobby's resolve

Opposite: The Attorney General had made a series of telephone calls to Governor Barnett and struck a deal to allow Meredith to register. When Barnett changed his mind, Bobby threatened to go public on the Governor's duplicity. Knowing that such revelations would damage him irreparably in the state, Barnett reluctantly capitulated. This was a classic example of Bobby's steely resolve and readiness to "play hardball."

Right: The President and First Lady are excited observers as the U.S. yacht *Weatherly* takes on *Gretel*, Australia's vessel, in the first of the races in the 1962 America's Cup.

Missile sites threaten United States

Above: The President entertains a delegation of Soviet officials, including Foreign Minister Andrei Gromyko (second right), on October 18. Three days earlier, a U-2 reconnaissance plane had revealed missile sites with an offensive capability, giving the lie to the Soviet line that the weapons were there purely for defensive reasons. Jack had the photographic evidence in his drawer during the two-hour meeting.

Left: On October 20, JFK informed the American people of the gravity of the situation, and said that if the Soviet Union did not begin dismantling the sites within 48 hours, a "quarantine line" would be placed around Cuba. This was effectively a blockade, but that term was not used because it was a potential breach of international law.

Right: West German Chancellor Konrad Adenauer delivers a speech, with JFK and Secretary of State Dean Rusk looking on. As the Cuban situation hung in the balance, the United States sent emissaries to several European countries to garner support. Adenauer, along with France's president de Gaulle, backed the United States' position. In the event, the Soviet Union shied away from crossing the line, which was a personal triumph for Jack.

Election success

Opposite: November 19, 1962. While Jackie enjoys a day's riding with the children, Jack delivered the long awaited "stroke of the pen" to outlaw discrimination in federally assisted housing. Late 1962 also saw progress on the issue of weapons inspections, which had been a stumbling block as far as nuclear test-ban treaty was concerned. The year ended with Jack and Jackie being feted in front of the 1,113 Cuban exiles whose release the President had negotiated. All these achievements played well with the electorate, and the Democrats were rewarded at the ballot box in the midterm Congressional elections.

Above: The Kennedys spent Christmas 1962 at Palm Beach, where they received the news that Joe's condition had worsened. He developed pneumonia, and on December 24 an emergency tracheotomy was performed to relieve his breathing. Jackie is pictured leaving the hospital after visiting her father-in-law.

Left: Jackie had given her husband total support during the crisis, but the cracks in their relationship reappeared after Jack invited Mary Meyer to a celebratory dinner at the White House.

CHAPTER SIX

Moral Maturity 1963

The beginning of 1963 was very different for the President and the First Lady. Jack was riding high in the opinion polls and was enjoying better health than he had for some time. He was also still conducting his affair with Mary Meyer. Jackie, by contrast, was at a low ebb. She discovered she was pregnant again, the joy tempered by concern over a possible miscarriage or complications. Even before the pregnancy was confirmed, she had decided to rein back her public duties. The rally at the Miami Orange Bowl at the end of 1962 would be the last event on such a scale that she would attend with her husband until the fateful trip to Dallas 11 months later. The refurbishment of the White House was largely complete, and there would be a void to fill. But in the past two years she felt she had discharged her PR duties as the President's consort. To the outside world he was now looking every inch the mature statesman. With her husband's image firmly established, Jackie saw it as no great hardship to leave the stage to him. She had no great fondness for the role of First Lady, and even the very term raised her hackles.

Her mood would not have been helped by the fact that Jack's affair with Meyer had been made public in a drunken outburst by a newspaperman at a press convention. Although it was kept out of print, the affair was now in the public domain. Jackie was well versed in remaining aloof from casual liaisons based purely on sex. This was something more, and thus more hurtful. Things came to a head in March. Jack decided to end his relationship with Meyer, although he would be drawn back to her within a matter of weeks.

Opposite: Jack emphasizes his point in 1963.

If domestic calm had been restored temporarily, Jack's administration was about to be rocked by the worst civil unrest ever seen in the United States. He was engaged in a battle of wills with Congress over plans to stimulate the economy with a $13.5 billion tax cut; the United States was already running a sizable deficit, and his proposals had not met with universal approval. However, fiscal policy soon became a secondary issue as blacks took their frustration onto the streets. Even the moderate tones of Martin Luther King Jr. became markedly more incensed at the lack of government action. Alabama was the flashpoint. Under the governorship of arch-segregationist George Wallace, it was the only state that refused to countenance integration at its state university in Tuscaloosa. On June 11, Wallace reluctantly stood aside to allow black students Vivian Malone and James Hood to enter the building, but made it clear that this was the loss of a battle, not of the war.

That evening, Jack made a groundbreaking speech, announcing that far-reaching civil rights legislation would be put before Congress within days. For the first time, he embraced the moral dimension of the issue, as King and others had long urged him to do. He invoked the Constitution itself, in which the equality of all individuals was a core tenet. The content of the speech and the passion with which it was delivered was thought to be too dangerous by some of his advisers. Kennedy ignored them, but he knew that presenting a civil rights bill to Congress and seeing it enacted were two very different things. The riots continued, with demonstrators unwilling to show the restraint Kennedy called for. Medgar Evers, a member of the National Association for the Advancement of Colored People, was murdered in Jackson, Mississippi. A week later, on the day of Evers' funeral, Kennedy's bill was presented before Congress. In his supporting speech he spoke of battlefield graveyards being color-blind. It was reminiscent of how he had defused the Catholic issue on the campaign trail by noting that nobody had asked him or his brother about their religious beliefs when they fought for their country. On August 28, more than 200,000 gathered at the Lincoln Memorial to hear an address by Dr. King Jr. He, too, referred to the Constitution, citing the famous words "We hold these truths to be self-evident, that all men are created equal." But his refrain, and his "dream," was that the fine words would be reflected in everyday society.

Despite the outstanding oratory of both men, the civil rights bill still hung in the balance in November 1963. It would eventually be passed in July the following year—it was left to Lyndon Johnson to preside over wide-ranging measures to end discrimination on grounds of race, color, sex, and religion. Kennedy would receive much posthumous credit for this landmark piece of legislation, but some maintain its successful passage was predicated on the wave of emotion that followed his assassination.

On June 10, the day before Kennedy spoke to the nation of the moral imperative of the civil rights issue, he made another keynote address at the American University, Washington. The theme was the "peace race"; during the Cuban crisis the previous fall, Jack had become aware of the hidden danger of radioactive fallout, which made him redouble his efforts to secure a test-ban treaty with Khrushchev, ignoring advisers who thought it would accomplish little other than to deliver a potentially fatal blow to hopes of reelection. Harold Macmillan had urged Jack to put morality before personal popularity or political gain, and in the memorable American University speech he did just that. Two months later, the two most powerful men on the planet agreed to establish a hotline connection. The Cuban crisis had revealed an inadequate and potentially dangerous system of communication between the two superpowers. Jack wanted to ensure that future security could not be jeopardized by poor communications.

The test-ban treaty was finally signed on October 7, 1963. Although it excluded underground testing, it was nevertheless an important first step in halting the arms race, and it stands as one of Kennedy's greatest achievements.

Relations between the superpowers were now less frosty, but only because of a shared understanding that the policy of mutual assured destruction was a cataclysmic threat to the present generation, and cast a long shadow over the future. In terms of ideology, there was accommodation, not reconciliation. Jack made that clear when he visited West Berlin at the end of June. He was visibly moved by seeing the Berlin Wall for the first time. It was a symbol of repression and subjugation, and he made freedom his theme: "All free men, wherever they may live, are citizens of Berlin, and therefore, as a free man, I take pride in the words 'Ich bin ein Berliner'."

On August 7, Jackie was rushed to hospital, where she underwent an emergency Cesarean. Patrick Bouvier Kennedy was born five weeks' premature. He had developed the same respiratory problem that had afflicted John and died two days later. Jack had arrived at the hospital too late for the birth, but it was he who held the baby's hand as he lost the fight for life. Jack had shielded Jackie from the gravity of the situation. He now faced her as a distraught father. In keeping with the new-found moral perspective, which now underpinned his political life, his reaction to the loss of a third child took on a new dimension. The contrast with the events of 1956 was stark. Jack's outpouring seems to have been a mixture of grief and guilt. The tragedy undoubtedly brought them closer than they had been for a long time.

In the fall of 1963, concern over events in Southeast Asia rose to the top of the political agenda. Jack had continued Eisenhower's policy of supporting South Vietnam's anti-Communist government, headed by Ngo Dinh Diem. Until now he had focused much of his attention on Cuba, Berlin, and Moscow. The persecution of Buddhists by the corrupt Catholic government changed all that, and presented Kennedy with a dilemma. He was worried about the inroads the Viet Cong were making, and the possibility of the country falling to Communism. However, he could not sanction the brutality of the Diem

Above: Jack preferred sports to high culture. Golf became a passion, although he was invariably hampered by his back problem.

regime. Shocking pictures of Buddhist monks who chose self-immolation over repression flashed around the world. Kennedy was receiving mixed messages from his advisers. Some recommended a full-scale military solution, while Jack inclined to those who had grave reservations about expanding U.S. involvement.

The South Vietnamese authorities were exhorted to clean up their act and to halt the oppression. When this fell on deaf ears, regime change emerged as an increasingly desirable outcome. Jack, still grieving over the death of his son and concerned over Jackie's well-being, was informed that a military coup in South

Vietnam was a real possibility. The rebel general wanted U.S. approval before acting, and Jack gave the green light, provided his top aides had no objection. Some of those advisers, including Secretary of State Dean Rusk, did indeed have objections, but deferred to what they believed was the President's view. Only after the plan was sanctioned did the misunderstanding come to light. Kennedy desperately tried to withdraw his approval, but the momentum was now unstoppable. The coup finally took place on November 1. Jack was worried that the insurrection might be laid at the United States' door, putting the improved relations with the Soviet Union at risk. Publicly, it was important to distance the United States from events in South Vietnam.

Above: At the Berlin Wall, June 26, 1963. Jack made his famous "Ich bin ein Berliner" speech in Rudolf-Wilde-Platz the same day.

Jack at least wanted Diem and his supporters to be treated with dignity, but matters were now out of his hands. He was appalled when he learned that Diem and his brother, Ngo Dinh Nhu, had been murdered. The immediate impact on the President was a powerful sense of personal responsibility. Since his father had become incapacitated, Jack had been much influenced by Macmillan, particularly when the exigencies of office brought morality and expediency into conflict. It is doubtful whether Joe Sr. would have anguished about Diem's fate.

In the fall of 1963, Jack's conduct as both president and husband could still be called into question. Indecisiveness and lack of judgment over Vietnam mirrored events surrounding the Bay of Pigs debacle. And despite his tender concerns over Jackie, he still couldn't give up Mary Meyer. However, at least he could now recognize a grievous wrong, both in his public and in his private life, and had the capacity to feel remorse and guilt.

How Kennedy would have dealt with the long-term ramifications of the coup in Vietnam remains a matter of conjecture. Some suggest he was intent on scaling back U.S. military involvement in the country; others that he passionately believed in maintaining a strong presence in the area, and that his commitment to winning the war was unshakable. One thing is clear. Following the events of November 22, the new president and his advisory team didn't appear to make any radical policy changes regarding U.S. involvement in Southeast Asia. Under Johnson, there was a huge escalation of American forces in this theater. It thus seems reasonable to suggest that JFK might have presided over a similar military buildup had he lived.

Jack's thoughts turned to the forthcoming election. Formulating policy on Southeast Asia or in any other area was academic if a second term could not be secured. Put another way, the pragmatist in him came to the forefront. The domestic economy was in good shape. In his handling of the Cold War and civil rights, he had managed to enhance his credentials with the Left without alienating

Below: Jack stands shoulder to shoulder with West Berlin's mayor, Willy Brandt, and Germany's Chancellor Konrad Adenauer. His unequivocal commitment to guarantee the divided city's freedom was greeted with rapturous enthusiasm by its people.

the Right. Vietnam was another potential banana skin, but he calculated that this issue could be held in abeyance without causing him significant electoral damage. Overall, conditions were favorable for another successful campaign, with Barry Goldwater his likely opponent.

A two-day visit to Texas was planned, one of the first ports of call in the long reelection campaign. A row had broken out between two leading Democrats, Governor John Connally and Senator Ralph Yarborough. Jack saw the visit as an opportunity to heal the rift between the two men, and to jump-start the 1964 campaign. It had been a long time since Jackie had accompanied her husband on a domestic political trip. Seeing how badly affected Jack had been by Diem's assassination, she decided to join him on the visit to Texas. It would be her first visit to the Lone Star state. It would be her husband's last.

A new dimension

Opposite above: The President ushers in the new year with a reception for labor and civil rights leaders, including Martin Luther King Jr. Jack was riding high in the opinion polls at the end of his second year in office. Until now his instincts had been to consolidate support and avoid risk. This year would be different: 1963 would see policy initiatives informed by a new moral dimension, even though he knew such actions jeopardized his chances of reelection.

Opposite below: January 14, 1963. Jackie watches her husband deliver his third State of the Union address, along with her mother, Janet Auchinloss, and sister Princess Lee Radziwill. For Jackie the year began on a joyous note as she discovered she was pregnant again. Having lost two babies, the happiness was tempered with trepidation. She was especially concerned in the early weeks of pregnancy, and the announcement was not made official until mid-April.

Above: Jack in ebullient mood as he outlines his views on how long politicians should be allowed to serve in office. He was already giving thought to what he would do after his days in the White House were over. One idea was for the creation of the John F. Kennedy Presidential Library at Harvard, and he was already having discussions with his alma mater about this prestigious project.

The price of glamour

Opposite: At a state dinner for the visit of Venezuela's president Rómulo Betancourt, Jackie's hairstyle receives as much attention as any political utterances. As usual, women throughout the country quickly copied any new look that Jackie adopted. However, the appearance came at a price. Designer outfits contributed to the $226,000 bill she ran up in her first two years as First Lady. Jack was not pleased and insisted that her spending was reined in, although he was estimated to be worth $10 million at the time.

Above: Jackie enjoys a night out at the theater with her sister and brother-in-law. The First Lady decided to drastically curtail her public engagements in 1963. After two years of notable achievement in discharging her duties, Jackie was eager to leave the stage to her husband. Pregnancy offered her the ideal excuse to make family considerations her main priority.

Left: Jack confers with Ted Sorensen, the man behind many of the memorable words Jack had spoken during the previous decade. Sorensen would soon be called upon to draft major speeches on civil rights and nuclear arms reduction, which would have the same kind of impact as the Inaugural Address of 1961.

Letter to Khrushchev

Left: April 24, 1963. Jack announces a breakthrough in the stalled negotiations with the Soviet Union over nuclear testing. Harold Macmillan had written to Kennedy a month earlier, urging him to do all he could to break the deadlock. The pressures on Jack were huge, both from the hawkish tendency within his own party and from the Republican opposition. Even if a treaty could be agreed, there was no guarantee that Congress would ratify it. Jack put these considerations aside, and both he and Macmillan were cosignatories to a letter sent to Khrushchev, indicating their willingness to resume talks.

Below: The President and First Lady enjoy a motorcade journey through Washington to mark the state visit of the King of Morocco. Jackie needed all her skills as a public performer for the visit, because she was in turmoil at the time. Jack's affair with Mary Meyer had been revealed in a drunken outburst by journalist Phil Graham at a press convention in Phoenix. This liaison caused Jackie increasing pain, because it went beyond the casual encounters that she had always tolerated.

Fielding questions

Above: The President exudes confidence as he fields journalists' questions at a news conference, April 1963. Jack had been studying a report documenting a century of struggle for America's black population. It was a shameful history of egregious acts of discrimination, much of it institutional. When many prominent black figures were invited to a White House reception, Jack showed he was still apprehensive about the issue. Sammy Davis Jr., entertainer and member of the famous "Rat Pack," attended with his Swedish wife, May Britt. Interracial marriages were still regarded by many as taboo, and Jack took care to ensure that the couple didn't pose together for the photographers.

Racial violence in Alabama

Opposite above: May 12, 1963. The President calls for calm as the tinderbox of Alabama threatens to ignite in a race war. Civil rights campaigners had been holding demonstrations in the state for the past month, protesting over blatant discriminatory policies that were endorsed by its arch-segregationist governor, George Wallace. Kennedy made it clear that if order was not restored, federal troops would be deployed.

Above: Jackie was eager to make an impact when she played hostess to the Grand Duke and Duchess of Luxembourg at the end of April. It was to be the last such White House reception she would preside over as First Lady before the birth of her baby. She invited the actor Basil Rathbone to put on a special performance, requesting him to recite the St. Crispin's Day speech from *Henry V*, a favorite of Jack's.

The Rometsch affair

Below: Bobby Kennedy and J. Edgar Hoover deep in consultation, with a major scandal brewing. Both men became aware that one of the President's casual partners, Ellen Rometsch, was also involved with a Soviet attaché. It was potentially as damaging as the Profumo affair, which was currently rocking the British government to its foundations. Jack quickly dropped Rometsch and she was subsequently deported. As late as the fall of 1963, RFK and Hoover were putting pressure on senators who were demanding an investigation into the affair. Had it not been for the events of November 22, the Rometsch scandal might have dealt a serious blow to the Kennedy administration.

A shared passion

Right: Jack and Jackie shared a passion for history, particularly the Civil War. In the spring of 1963, they visited a number of historic sites, including Gettysburg, where they engaged in good-humored banter as to whose knowledge of the period was greater. For some three months, Jackie was buoyed by the thought that her husband had ended his relationship with Mary Meyer. She also had the boost of moving the family out of the Kennedy compound at Hyannis Port, which she had never liked. Their new home on Cape Cod was Brambletyde, Squaw Island, a short distance from the compound. Jack liked the property, chiefly because of its proximity to the ocean. He was less taken with Jackie's other pet project, their new house in Virginia. He was also angry that having spent a lot of money redecorating Glen Ora, they had to pay a huge sum to restore it to its original condition when the lease was up.

President invokes Constitution on civil rights issue

Left: May 18, 1963. Jack meets Peace Corps workers bound for Indonesia. The Peace Corps remained one of the administration's success stories, and Kennedy's interest in international affairs was undiminished. However, the wave of violence in Alabama occupied his thoughts, and later the same day he gave an impassioned speech on civil rights at Vanderbilt University, Tennessee. The rioting continued, and there were shocking pictures of the police turning their dogs loose on the protestors, a move sanctioned by Police Chief "Bull" Connor. Kennedy responded by invoking the Constitution itself, which held equality as a core tenet. A civil rights bill was drafted and put before Congress the following month.

Above: Jackie introduces John Jr. to astronaut Gordon Cooper, who had just been presented with the Distinguished Service Medal at a White House ceremony. John Jr. was fascinated by flight. When Jack's helicopter landed, father and son would often spend time playing at the controls together. Kite flying was another favorite pastime, and Jack kept toy planes in the Oval Office for when his son came to play. Jackie was the inspiration behind Caroline's main passion, riding horses.

Opposite: Jackie's renovation of the White House included a lot of work on the grounds, especially the Rose Garden. As a surprise gift for their forthcoming tenth anniversary, Jackie began work on a scrapbook of the restoration work.

The White House school

Left: Jackie and Caroline at the White House kindergarten, late spring 1963. Jackie was heavily involved in the setting up of the school, anxious to give her children as normal an upbringing as possible. It eventually had ten pupils and was staffed by qualified teachers. The public loved domestic images of the First Family, and there was huge media interest in Jackie's pregnancy. The fall would see a dramatic turnaround, with Jackie subjected to some vitriolic abuse from both the press and the public.

Below: Jackie and John Jr. with other Kennedy family members at the White House, May 24, 1963. Five days later, in celebration of Jack's 46th birthday, Jackie organized a trip down the Potomac on the yacht *Sequoia*. Mary Meyer joined the party, something Jackie accepted with equanimity as Meyer was now seeing one of Jack's aides. She would be devastated shortly afterward when it became clear that Jack had resumed his affair with her.

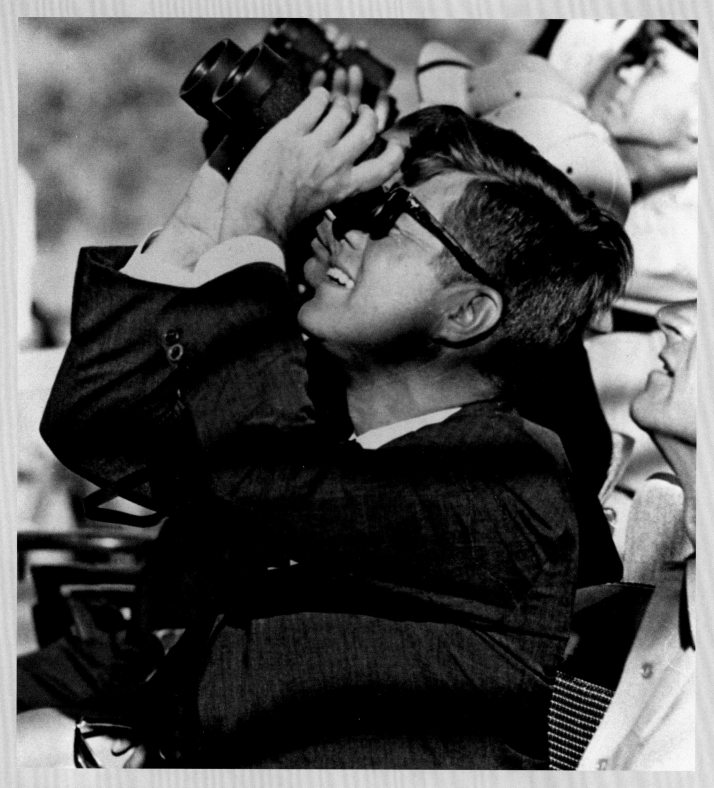

Khrushchev agrees to test-ban talks

Above: The President tracks a missile launched at the White Sands missile range in New Mexico. Shortly afterward, Khrushchev gave a positive reply to the letter he and Macmillan had sent, and it was agreed that high-level talks between the superpowers would take place in July. The news came through during a five-day domestic trip, which included a visit to Texas. There he met Governor John Connally and Senator Ralph Yarborough, the protagonists in some bitter infighting between rival Democratic factions. The differences between the two were unresolved, and Jack agreed to return to the Lone Star state before the end of the year.

"Ich bin ein Berliner"

Opposite below: June 26, 1963. Jack addresses a huge West Berlin crowd at Rudolf-Wilde-Platz. His speech contrasted democracy and freedom with the repression of Communist regimes: "Freedom has many difficulties and democracy is not perfect, but we have never had to put a wall up to keep our people in, to prevent them from leaving us." He pointed out that freedom was absolute, not relative, and the subjugation of one man was a denial of freedom to all: "All free men, wherever they may live, are citizens of Berlin, and therefore, as a free man, I take pride in the words 'Ich bin ein Berliner'."

Opposite above: Against the backdrop of the Brandenburg Gate, the presidential party, including Robert and Ethel Kennedy and West Berlin's mayor, Willy Brandt, gets a first-hand view of the Berlin Wall, constructed two years earlier. The East Berlin authorities draped the arches of the famous portal in red cloth to prevent the dignitaries from looking into their territory.

Above: The President fields questions at a press conference in Bonn, June 25, 1963. He reaffirms his unwavering support for West Berlin. The sight of the Wall had affected him deeply, bringing his "cold warrior" instincts to the forefront.

Ireland welcomes a son

Opposite: After the highly charged political visit to Germany, the next leg of Kennedy's European tour had more personal resonance. There were chaotic scenes in Cork, Ireland, where the people turned out in droves to catch a glimpse of a world leader whose roots lay in their homeland.

Left: Mary Ryan, a distant relative of Jack's, steps up to plant a kiss on the presidential cheek. At one point, when the crush threatened to become overwhelming, security men stepped forward to intervene. Jack waved them away with the words, "It's all right, these are my people."

Below: Jack and his sister, Eunice Shriver, visit the ancestral home of the Kennedy clan in Dunganstown, County Wexford. It was from here that Jack's great-grandfather Patrick Kennedy had emigrated to the United States in 1848. Jackie tried to incorporate the Kennedy roots into their new home in Virginia, renaming it "Wexford."

The family gather

Left: July 19, 1963. A family gathering at Hyannis Port to mark the christening of the newest family member. Patricia Lawford holds Christopher George Kennedy, Bobby and Ethel's eighth child, who had been christened by Cardinal Richard Cushing at St. Francis Xavier Church. Jack was looking forward to repeating the ceremony after the birth of his third child. In the meantime, he was preoccupied by the nuclear test-ban talks, which had begun in Moscow four days earlier. Underground testing looked like being the sticking point, and Jack instructed his envoy, Averell Harriman, to secure a deal just on atmospheric testing if a total ban wasn't possible. Macmillan had urged this course of action as a very worthy second prize. Agreement was finally reached at the end of the month.

The President relaxes

Left: Jack was an enthusiastic if not very accomplished golfer. Back pain often restricted his ability to play, but in July 1963 he was feeling better than he had for some time. He spent much of the month at Brambletyde, where Jackie was filling her time reading and painting while awaiting the birth of their child. The brazen way in which Jack had renewed his affair with Mary Meyer hit Jackie hard. It appeared as deliberate and callous as the way in which Joe Kennedy flaunted his mistresses before Rose. He was also a concerned expectant father, however, and Jackie became even more anxious that her pregnancy should proceed normally.

"A victory for mankind"

Above: July 26, 1963. The President broadcasts to the nation, describing the signing of the nuclear test-ban treaty as "a victory for mankind." The agreement prohibited testing in the atmosphere, underwater, and in space. Underground testing was excluded from the deal, but Kennedy still regarded this first major step along the disarmament road as one of his greatest achievements.

Opposite below: Jackie, seven months pregnant, takes the strain out of accompanying her husband around the golf course at Newport, Rhode Island. She had already begun organizing the baby's room and making arrangements for the christening. On July 28, there was a more immediate cause for family celebration as Jackie celebrated her 34th birthday.

United in grief

Opposite: The President and his son receive the unwarranted attention of photographers as they visit Jackie in hospital. She had been rushed in on August 7, complaining of abdominal pain. An emergency Cesarean was performed and a 4-pound 10-ounce boy was born, five weeks premature. Jack had immediately flown from Andrews Air Force Base when he heard the news, but his son was born before he arrived at the hospital. Patrick Bouvier Kennedy had hyaline membrane disease, the same respiratory problem that had afflicted John Jr. He died on August 9. This was John Jr's first visit since his mother was taken into hospital. He was too young to take in what had happened; Caroline, on the other hand, was looking forward to having a baby brother or sister, and was deeply upset when her father broke the news.

Above: Jack and Jackie leave Otis Air Force Base Hospital on August 14, five days after Patrick's death. Many commentators noted the fact that they left for Squaw Island hand in hand, as Jackie usually trailed behind her husband when they were walking together in public. The unity that this change suggested was genuine: the loss of their child had a profound effect on their relationship.

Family responsibilities

Above: A tired Caroline cuddles up to her father aboard the yacht *Marlin*, summer 1963. A few days before Jackie was rushed into hospital, Jack had surprised the family by bringing home some puppies. His attempt to divert the children, who were becoming restless waiting for the new arrival, helped in the weeks following Patrick's death. Jack needed no such distraction. He made regular shuttle trips between Washington and Cape Cod to see Jackie. He appeared to take the loss even harder than his wife, because he had guilt and remorse to contend with, as well as grief.

Left: Jack accompanies John Jr., Caroline, and their cousins to the store at Hyannis Port.

Opposite: John Jr. plays at being skipper, late August 1963. He was intelligent and talkative, endlessly fascinated by the world around him, particularly all things mechanical.

War against organized crime

Left: The Attorney General testifies before a Senate committee on organized crime. RFK's war on the Mafia was certainly not the accommodation the mobsters expected after their "contribution" to the 1960 election victory. When the President's connection with Judith Campbell—and thus Sam Giancana—was revealed in 1975, many believed it strengthened the case that the Mafia was behind the events in Dallas. This was further fueled when Giancana himself was murdered the same year.

Jackie heads for Europe

Opposite below: October 1, 1963. The President and First Lady greet Emperor Haile Selassie of Ethiopia at Union Station, Washington. The 73-year-old Lion of Judah was yet another world leader who fell under Jackie's spell, despite the fact that the First Lady was at a low ebb and desperate to leave for Europe. Her sister Lee had invited her to join a party on board Aristotle Onassis's yacht *Christina*. Lee's affair with the buccaneering tycoon was providing the gossip columnists with a rich source of material.

Above: Receiving Emperor Haile Selassie was Jackie's first official engagement since Patrick's death seven weeks earlier. She left for Greece during the state banquet given in honor of the Ethiopian leader's visit. Jack had reservations about the trip. It had already attracted a lot of adverse publicity, something that had always been an important benchmark for him. On this occasion, his concern for Jackie's welfare overrode public relations considerations.

Public anger over late-night reveling

Left: Jackie on vacation in Greece, October 1963. The wave of public sympathy for the First Lady after the loss of her baby turned to anger when details of her trip were published. Stanislaus Radziwill, along with F. D. Roosevelt Jr. and his wife, had joined the party at Jack's behest, but it failed to have the desired effect. There were rumors about impropriety, but the tender love letters Jackie wrote while she was away suggest otherwise. The First Lady seemed reinvigorated when she returned, and soon decided she wanted to play an active role in Jack's reelection campaign. She agreed to accompany her husband on his forthcoming visit to Texas, her first domestic political trip as First Lady.

Below: In addition to the bad publicity surrounding the First Lady's European trip, the President had many weighty political matters to occupy him in early October. He met with Britain's Foreign Secretary Lord Home as the situation in South Vietnam was reaching a crisis point. A matter of days later, Jack's close political ally Harold Macmillan resigned from office, and Alec Douglas-Home replaced him as Britain's prime minister.

Opposite: October 7, 1963. The President signs the nuclear test-ban treaty, a historic first step on the road to ending the arms race. Kennedy described it as "a message of hope for all the world."

Misunderstanding on South Vietnam

Left: November 1, 1963. Events in Saigon go to the top of the political agenda as Jack is awakened with the news that a coup has unseated South Vietnam's leader Ngo Dinh Diem. South Vietnam had enjoyed American support but persecution of the country's Buddhists had led to many horrifying acts of self-immolation. In late August, the President, distracted by grief, gave tacit approval for a military coup. He did so believing his top advisers thought this was the best course of action. They, in turn, consented, thinking they were carrying out the President's orders. By the time the misunderstanding came to light, events in South Vietnam had taken on a momentum of their own, culminating in the overthrow of Diem on November 1.

Opposite: Jack regularly took to his rocking chair to help relieve his back pain. UN Ambassador Adlai Stevenson had just returned from a trip to Dallas, where he received an extremely hostile reception. Placards of the President bearing the legend "Wanted For Treason" had been brandished, an indication that many of the citizens there regarded the recent test-ban treaty as a sellout. These events are said to have left the President in a fatalistic mood as his own trip to Texas approached.

Below: Rose Kennedy gives a forthright television interview on the subject of disabled children. The family had long dissembled on the subject of Rosemary, who had in fact been at St. Coletta's School, Jefferson, Wisconsin, since 1949.

Jack's moral dimension

Below: The bond between Jack and Jackie was stronger than ever in the fall of 1963. With Jackie intent on playing an active campaigning role in 1964, the future looked bright. Jack's popularity rating with the voters was higher than ever, and with the First Lady adding her singular appeal, it presented a formidable obstacle for the likely Republican candidate, Barry Goldwater. The first hurdle was the Texas trip, however, and Jack was eager to get that out of the way, particularly the visit to Dallas, widely regarded as the most anti-Democratic city in the country.

Left: Jack smiles as John Jr. skips after attending a ceremony at Arlington National Cemetery in November 1963.

Opposite: Jack in pensive mood, two days before the Texas trip. He had just paid what was to be his last visit to his father. In the two years since Joe's debilitating stroke, Jack's decisions had become increasingly informed by a new moral dimension. Joe's mantra, to do whatever it took to succeed, had got Jack to the White House. It was no longer his way, either in his public or in his personal life. Harold Macmillan undoubtedly played a key role in bringing out Jack's core decency, a determination to do the right thing, even if it went against self-interest.

CHAPTER SEVEN

Dallas
November 22, 1963

There was a sense of foreboding in the Kennedy camp about the trip to Dallas. UN Ambassador Adlai Stevenson had visited the city the previous month and been given a hostile reception. Even Lyndon Johnson, one of the state's own sons, had fallen from favor, and there were no guarantees that his presence on the ticket for 1964 would reap electoral rewards. Texas was an important part of the reelection campaign, and to visit the state and not go to Dallas was unthinkable.

The whistle-stop tour was to take in five venues over two days. On the morning of November 22, the Kennedys left Fort Worth for Dallas, the fourth leg of the trip. Things had gone well so far, the President and First Lady having been warmly received in San Antonio and Houston. There had been concerns that Jackie might be given a torrid time following a recent solo trip to Greece. She had received a lot of bad press over alleged revelry aboard Aristotle Onassis's yacht. According to reports, such behavior ill became a woman who had so recently lost a child and whose husband was faced with such weighty affairs of state. However, these fears were quickly dispelled. Jackie carefully chose some conservative outfits for the Texas trip. This was a hedge against criticism that she was too fond of haute couture and life's luxuries, and lacked the common touch. Even so, she was the epitome of glamour and style and won the crowds over wherever she went. Halfway through the visit reports were already praising Jackie's sure-footed performance on the political stage

Left: Jackie is presented with a bouquet of roses as cheering crowds greet the Kennedys at Love Field, Dallas, November 22, 1963.

and declaring her to be the jewel in the crown as far as her husband's reelection hopes were concerned.

The couple left Fort Worth for Dallas in buoyant mood. Thirteen minutes later, Air Force One touched down at Love Field and the President and First Lady were soon working a highly receptive crowd. At 11:55 they took their places on the raised rear seat of the Lincoln convertible. Governor Connally and his wife Nellie sat on the jump seats opposite. It was a bright, clear day and the vehicle's bulletproof bubble had been removed.

The motorcade made its way through the city, greeted enthusiastically by the crowds that lined the streets. The destination was the Trade Mart, where Jack was to make a speech. As the Lincoln turned into Dealey Plaza, three shots rang out. The first bullet struck Jack in the back. Before Secret Servicemen could reach the vehicle, the second bullet hit him in the back of the head. Governor Connally was also shot and seriously wounded. Jackie cradled her husband's head as the car sped to Parkland Hospital, just a few minutes' drive away. Kennedy's heart was still beating and the trauma team attempted a tracheotomy. However, with virtually the entire right side of the brain now missing, it was a hopeless task. John F. Kennedy was declared dead at 1:00 p.m.

The security men who first attended the President knew there was no hope. The injuries were so appalling that some instinctively ran to Lyndon Johnson's car, which was some way behind the President's in the motorcade. Ninety-eight minutes after Kennedy was pronounced dead, Johnson took the 40-word oath of office and was sworn in as the 36th President of the United States. The brief ceremony

Above: Lyndon and Lady Bird Johnson comfort Jackie , who refused to change out of the blood-splattered suit.

Opposite: The grieving family leave the Capitol building.

took place aboard Air Force One, which was taking both him and Kennedy's body back to Washington. Jackie stood beside Johnson as he took the oath, her clothes still spattered with her husband's blood and tissue.

Within a matter of hours the police had a suspect in custody. Lee Harvey Oswald, a 24-year-old former marine, had lived in the Soviet Union between 1959 and 1962. He worked as a clerk at the Texas School Book Depository on Elm Street, and police quickly concluded that this was the building from which the shots had been fired. A carbine and three empty shells were discovered on the sixth floor, and the weapon was traced back to Oswald. He was charged with murder, although rumors of a larger conspiracy began circulating almost immediately.

On November 24, Oswald himself was shot and killed while being moved from the local police station to the state prison. In the two days he had spent in custody, he

had not confessed to firing the gun that killed Kennedy and wounded Connally. The man who shot him was Jack Ruby, a Dallas nightclub owner. Ruby was arrested and later convicted of Oswald's murder.

President Johnson set up a commission under Chief Justice Earl Warren to investigate the events of November 22. The report was delivered ten months later, in September 1964, and it concluded that Oswald had acted alone. Ruby had perpetrated an individual act of revenge. In short, there was no wider conspiracy. These findings did nothing to end speculation. Between them Jack and Bobby had peered into some murky waters and made many enemies. They had taken on Jimmy Hoffa and the Teamsters Union; there had been dubious connections with the Mafia; Castro and the Kremlin also came under suspicion, while some thought it more than coincidental that the assassination followed so closely on the heels of Diem's murder in South Vietnam. Bobby was among the first to wonder if the CIA were implicated.

Rumors persisted for 15 years, when the House Select Committee on Assassinations finally shed new light on what happened in Dallas. Acoustics experts suggested that shots were fired from the grassy knoll on Dealey Plaza, as well as from the book depository. The identity of the perpetrators was—and remains—a mystery, but the theory of a disaffected individual was finally disproved.

John F. Kennedy took office determined to make his mark on history. Lyndon Johnson accepted the vice presidency wondering whether yet another first executive would die in office and propel him into the top job. The events of Dallas on November 22, 1963, turned conjecture into reality for both men.

For a long time, accounts of John F. Kennedy's life and work became more akin to hagiography. His premature and violent death meant that his good qualities and achievements were magnified, his shortcomings and failures overlooked. The fact is that until November 1960 he knew more about how to win power than what to do with it. After taking office, he found that the learning curve was steep, and there were many reverses along the way. He grew in stature during his 1,000-day tenure of the White House, and by the time of his death, he was on the threshold of greatness.

However, the balance-sheet approach fails to take account of the emotional impact Kennedy had, both on the American people and on those beyond its shores. Through the world he envisioned, the ideals he espoused, described as they were so memorably, he touched people's lives in a way few statesmen have managed to do, either before or since. He was more than an inspiring politician; he symbolized the hopes and dreams of a generation.

Breakfast in Texas

Left: The President joins in the applause for the First Lady at a Chamber of Commerce breakfast, Fort Worth, on the morning of Friday, November 22, 1963. The Kennedys had arrived at 11 p.m. the previous evening, having earlier visited San Antonio and Houston. Jack had already made one impromptu speech that morning, going down to the hotel parking lot to greet the assembled well-wishers. The crowd wanted Jackie, to which the President responded: "Mrs. Kennedy is organizing herself. It takes a little longer but, of course, she looks better than we do when she does it." The President's visit was not met with universal good humor. The *Dallas Morning News* had a lot of barbed comment, including a full-page advertisement welcoming the President— surrounded by a black border. When Jack saw the hostile press reports, he declared that he and Jackie were in "nut country."

A fateful decision

Above: Jackie sits between the President and Governor John Connally as the motorcade journey gets under way. As they made their way into Dallas, Connally took his place in the jump seat opposite, next to his wife. Jack told Jackie to concentrate her attention on the crowd lining the street to her left, while he acknowledged those on his side; it was unnecessary duplication for both to woo the same voter. Jackie wanted to wear sunglasses to shield her eyes from the blinding sun. Ever the politician, Jack realized the importance of eye contact and asked her to remove them. These were the last words he spoke to her.

Opposite above: The glorious weather meant that the presidential Lincoln had its bulletproof bubble removed. Behind came four police motorcyclists and a limousine carrying several Secret Service personnel. On the running boards were agents Hill and Ready, who were charged with the protection of the President and First Lady, respectively.

The final journey

Right: The famous image of Jackie cradling her husband as he slumps in his seat. The first bullet struck the President in the back of the neck, exited the throat, and hit Governor Connally. The second shattered Kennedy's skull. He was still alive on arrival at Parkland Memorial Hospital but there was no hope that he could have survived such terrible injuries.

"I want them to see what they have done"

Above: Jackie witnesses the swearing in of Lyndon Baines Johnson as 36th President of the United States. The brief ceremony took place aboard Air Force One, which then left for Washington. JFK's body was in the rear of the plane. Hurried phone calls had been made to ascertain who had the authority to administer the 40-word oath. Bobby Kennedy himself was consulted in his role as Attorney General. He confirmed that U.S. District Judge Sarah Hughes could perform the ceremony. Johnson officially took office 98 minutes after JFK was pronounced dead. The relationship between the Johnsons and the Kennedys was cool at best, but Jackie had always got on well with the Vice President. She refused to change out of her blood-spattered pink woolen suit, declaring, "I want them to see what they have done."

Opposite below: Jackie accompanies her husband's body to Bethesda Naval Hospital, where the mandatary autopsy was to be performed. It was there that Bobby met her. He had been at his Hickory Hill home when news of his brother's death came through. He had spent the morning in meetings to do with the ongoing war on organized crime. When the lone gunman theory was eventually discredited, there was much speculation regarding Mafia involvement.

Opposite above: RFK and some of his children, pictured shortly after he was informed of his brother's death. Bobby was the mainstay of the family in the aftermath of the tragedy. He was both practical and a source of great emotional support to others, although inconsolable himself.

"He belongs to the country"

Above: Sunday November 24. Members of the Kennedy family stand together at the Capitol Rotunda to listen to a eulogy for the late President. By the next morning, a quarter of a million people had filed past the casket. The protocol for lying-in-state was for the casket to remain open, but Jackie felt her husband's body, drained of blood, looked like a waxwork figure and refused. She also stood firm on the choice of burial place. The Kennedy clan favored the family plot at Brookline. It was Jackie who insisted on the national cemetery at Arlington, commenting: "He belongs to the country."

Opposite: Jackie holds the flag that was draped over her husband's coffin. She won universal admiration for the stoicism and dignity with which she bore her loss. Many described her deportment and demeanor on the day of the funeral as regal.

A poignant moment

Following pages: At his mother's prompting, John Jr. executed a faultless salute after the service at St. Matthew's Cathedral. Previously, he had never quite managed to get it right. The day of the funeral was John Jr.'s third birthday. Caroline was six two days later, November 27, 1963. Breaking with tradition, Jackie insisted on walking behind the gun carriage, which bore the casket. A riderless black horse followed, with a sheathed sword and boots reversed in the stirrups, indicating that a commander-in-chief had fallen. President de Gaulle, Haile Selassie, and Prince Philip, Duke of Edinburgh, were among the dignitaries in attendance. One notable absentee was Jack's mentor and friend, Harold Macmillan, who was too ill to travel.

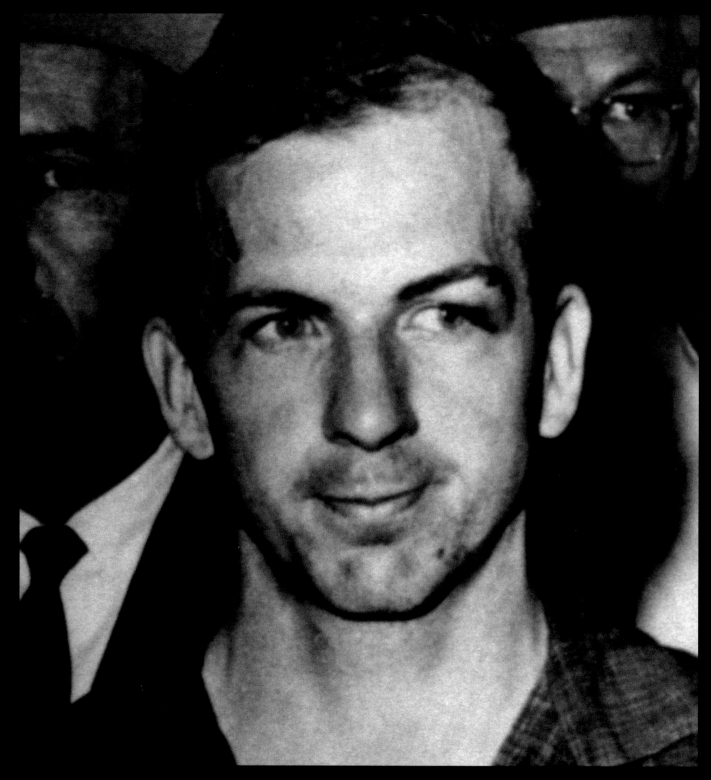

Oswald charged

Above: Within hours of Kennedy's assassination, Lee Harvey Oswald was arrested and charged with murder. A 24-year-old disaffected former marine, Oswald worked at the Texas School Book Depository, the building which had housed the assassin, according to Dallas Police. Oswald himself was shot by nightclub owner Jack Ruby on Sunday, November 24, while he was being transferred to the county jail. He died 48 hours later at Parkland Memorial Hospital, having been attended by some of the same doctors who had fought to save the President. In the two days he spent in custody he did not confess to Kennedy's murder.

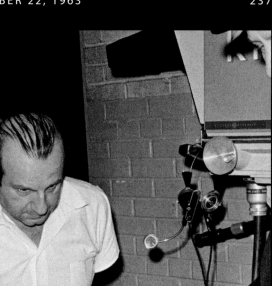

Ruby jailed

Above: On the day of JFK's funeral, Jack Ruby is transferred from Dallas city jail to the county facility.

Right: This photograph was a key exhibit in the Warren Commission's investigation into the events of November 22, 1963. It shows Oswald holding the same Mannlicher-Carcano rifle that was found on the sixth floor of the Texas School Book Depository. The 10-month inquiry produced a 10-million-word report with a simple conclusion: that both Oswald and Ruby had acted alone. It was later alleged that the photograph of Oswald was a fake, and in 1978 acoustics experts suggested that there had been a second gunman. The following year, the doubts raised led the House Assassinations Committee to conclude that the President had been the victim of a wider conspiracy, although the identity of the perpetrators remained a mystery.

CHAPTER EIGHT

Passing of the Torch

1963–

The death of John F. Kennedy—the fourth American president to fall victim to an assassin's bullet—sent shock waves around the world. It was an event of national and international significance; it was also yet another crushing blow to the family, absorbed with customary fortitude. The Kennedy way was to endure and move on, not to yield or wallow. Jackie, who insisted upon walking behind her husband's casket on the way to its final resting place, was from the same mold. When the grieving was over, the former First Lady had to look to the future with her two young children. Meanwhile, there were two Kennedy brothers still in the front line of politics. Robert Kennedy's presidential ambitions were formed soon after his brother's assassination. It was widely held to be merely a matter of time before he sought the highest office to carry forward the dynastic torch and fulfill JFK's unrealized aims. Lineage and unfinished business was his theme when he began his term as Senator in 1965, having resigned from the post of Attorney General the previous year. "We started something in 1960," he said, "and the vote today is an overwhelming mandate to continue."

Joining Ted, a senator since 1962, Bobby endorsed liberal measures, such as the Voting Rights Act and anti-poverty programs. The hopes of the younger generation were now pinned on a man who showed his credentials as champion of the underprivileged. He was a constant thorn in President

Johnson's side—there was no love lost between the two— not least over U.S. involvement in Vietnam, a war Bobby came to believe unwinnable.

Early in 1968 Kennedy spoke of the malaise in the country, particularly among a disengaged youth "turned on with drugs and turned off America." He questioned the country's standing in the world, whether it still commanded respect, and noted the folly of "flaunting our power and wealth against the judgment and desires of neutrals and allies alike." The United States was mired in a war halfway around the world that millions of its citizens repudiated. Deprivation and despair could be found on their own doorstep. In a presidential election year, he invited the public to consider not simply who the nation's next chief executive should be, but in which direction it ought to be going.

Kennedy said he could not envisage circumstances in which he would oppose Lyndon Johnson for the Democratic nomination. Perhaps 1972 afforded the better chance for the clear heir apparent, for there were risks in taking on the White House incumbent. However, Senator Eugene McCarthy's strong showing in the early primaries exposed Johnson's vulnerability; it meant Kennedy could enter the race without being blamed for creating divisions in the party. In April 1968—by which time LBJ had decided not to seek a second term—Kennedy was polling well ahead of McCarthy, although the still-undeclared Vice President Hubert Humphrey enjoyed significant support. Days later, Humphrey formally entered the fray. RFK's campaign gathered momentum, his supporters smelling victory after successes in the Indiana and Nebraska primaries. There was

Left: Bobby pressing the flesh during the 1968 presidential campaign. He joked wryly that he was reviled equally by big business and organized labor, but to the country's youth he offered the promise of a brighter future.

a setback as McCarthy carried Oregon, but it was still all to play for as the political bandwagon moved to California.

In what proved to be his final bout of campaigning, Kennedy warned against the country assuming the role of world policeman. He restated his pledge to end the war in Vietnam, and he came out strongly in support of military aid for Israel. The latter policy inflamed the passions of 24-year-old Jerusalem-born Palestinian Sirhan Sirhan, whose family had arrived in the United States a decade earlier. Sirhan was among the jubilant throng of Kennedy supporters celebrating their man's victory in the key California primary at the Ambassador Hotel in Los Angeles on June 4, 1960, a result that effectively knocked McCarthy out of the race. Shortly after midnight, Kennedy left the ballroom stage where he had given a rousing speech and was ushered away through the hotel kitchen en route to a press conference. There was a burst of gunfire and Robert Francis Kennedy fell, succumbing to grievous injuries some 24 hours later. He was 42 years old and his wife Ethel pregnant with their eleventh child at the time of his death. Teddy, the sole surviving brother, gave a moving eulogy at the funeral service, speaking of a man "who saw wrong and tried to right it, saw suffering and tried to heal it, saw

war and tried to stop it." A nation's hopes, for the second time in five years, had been struck a bitter blow. Robert Kennedy was laid to rest at Arlington National Cemetery, near his brother.

At his trial Sirhan Sirhan said the crime was committed "with 20 years of malice aforethought," a reference to the founding of the State of Israel. In a journal, he had noted that Kennedy had to be killed by June 5, 1968—the first anniversary of the Six Day War. He was sentenced to death but was subsequently commuted to life in prison when California abolished capital punishment. In 2011, his fourteenth parole application was rejected.

Almost inevitably, conspiracy theories abound with regard to the second member of the Kennedy clan to fall victim to an assassin's bullet. If those concerning CIA involvement or Manchurian Candidate-type mind manipulation are rejected, there are eyewitness accounts asserting the presence of a second gunman—an eerie echo of events in Dallas. Kennedy was shot at point-blank range from behind—one bullet struck the back of his head—whereas Sirhan was said to be in front of the senator as the latter made his way through the hotel kitchen. Witnesses, backed up by acoustics experts, have also attested that more than eight shots were fired—beyond the capacity of Sirhan's weapon. Speculation persists.

Bobby's death meant Joseph and Rose Kennedy had outlived four of their nine children. Joe, who had a massive stroke in 1961, died 18 months after his third son, leaving Rose to preside as family matriarch for another 25 years. She died in January 1995, at the age of 104.

The assassination of Robert Kennedy had a profound effect on his sister-in-law. Camelot's queen had rebuilt her life since that fateful day in Dallas, her stoicism in grief endearing her even more to the American people. Jackie had fought depression—Bobby providing much comfort and support—and realized that a 34-year-old widow with

Left: June 9, 1968. Jackie and children at Bobby Kennedy's grave, Arlington National Cemetery, Virginia. Jackie had been reinvigorated at the prospect of Bobby becoming president. His violent death hastened her decision to exchange America for marriage to Onassis and the security of Skorpios.

two children had to look beyond glorifying her husband's achievements and preserving his memory. It was she who turned Bobby's idea for renaming Cape Canaveral, the Kennedy Space Center, and Idlewild Airport, JFK Airport, into a reality. President Johnson not only acceded to those requests but offered Jackie an ambassadorial role, which she declined.

After briefly setting up home in Georgetown, which became a goldfish-bowl attraction, Jackie headed to New York, just as Bobby was moving there to further his political ambitions. She fell back on her usual occupations: riding, shopping, decorating, and travel. There were also romances, her suitors including David Ormsby-Gore, Britain's ambassador to Washington, with whom both she and Jack had been good friends. Jackie's life became more settled, and she was positively rejuvenated when Bobby decided to run for president in the spring of 1968. His death left her traumatized. These were violent times to be living in, and

Below: Caroline, Jackie and John Jr. pictured during a family vacation in Ireland, June 1967.

soon the ideal escape route presented itself in the shape of buccaneering tycoon Aristotle Onassis. Their marriage, in October 1968, offered Jackie the security she craved, while the rough-hewn magnate landed a prize socialite, one of the world's most glamorous women. It was a union that shocked many; Jackie's saintly public image was tarnished when she became mistress of Skorpios.

Onassis, an inveterate womanizer, was not the kind to embrace monogamy. Unfaithfulness, however, was not a deal breaker because both got what they wanted from the relationship, initially at least. However, the marriage had foundered long before Onassis's death in 1975. He was acquisitive and easily bored, a Lothario with an aging wife. For her part, Jackie missed her homeland; being a free spirit was not part of the lot of a Greek wife. And despite his enormous wealth, he also took umbrage at her lavish spending. Superstition also played a part. The Onassis family was struck by a series of family tragedies, including the death of the tycoon's beloved son Alexander. There were business problems, too, and some laid the ill fortune at Jackie's door.

Whether or not Onassis believed she was a harbinger of bad luck, he wanted out of the marriage and began angling to mitigate the financial impact of divorce. When he died of myasthenia gravis, the settlement became the subject of a protracted lawsuit, Jackie eventually beginning a new chapter back in New York, keeping Onassis's name and $26 million of his fortune.

She took up residence on Fifth Avenue, and also acquired a 400-acre estate on Martha's Vineyard. She also landed an editing job with Viking Press, her first paid employment since the brief flirtation with photojournalism some 25 years earlier. Inevitably, her celebrity preceded her, and there were those who questioned whether her value lay in who she was rather than what she could do. In 1978, Jackie was appointed to a similar role at Doubleday Books, where she strove to maintain a low profile and was accepted simply as a member of the team. Highly regarded for her dedication to her work and sedulous attention to detail, she remained with the publishing house until her final illness.

Jackie's later years brought lasting romance with Maurice Tempelsman, a financier and diamond merchant whom she had known since her days as First Lady. He lacked the scintillating presence and raw appeal of her two husbands, but as Jackie turned 50 in 1979, his qualities of dependability and gentleness more than compensated. The two were able to converse in French and shared a love of the arts. Tempelsman was married and for a long time their affair remained clandestine. He and his wife separated in 1982, and Tempelsman eventually moved into Jackie's Fifth Avenue apartment. They did not marry.

Tempelsman's devotion to Jackie extended to her children. By now, however, Jackie was eager to see Caroline and John making their own way in the world, free of any

Below: Jackie and Teddy remained close despite the fact that their lives diverged during the former's self-imposed exile and marriage to Aristotle Onassis.

family encumbrances. In 1980, Caroline graduated from Radcliffe College, Harvard, with a degree in fine arts and took up employment in the media department of the Metropolitan Museum of Art. In 1986, Caroline married Edwin Schlossberg, whom she met while working at the Museum, their nuptials overshadowing the other high-profile family wedding of the year, that between Maria Shriver—the second of Eunice Kennedy and Sargent Shriver's five children—and movie star Arnold Schwarzenegger. Schlossberg was intelligent and cultured—and 13 years her senior, almost exactly the age difference there had been between her parents. In 1988, Caroline gave birth to a daughter, Rose, while studying for a law degree during her pregnancy. Tatiana arrived soon afterward, and in January 1993, she gave birth to John, who inevitably would be known as Jack.

John Jr.—who stole a nation's heart with his perfectly executed salute at his father's funeral—had a varied career. He graduated from Brown University, Providence, Rhode Island, where he majored in American history. He went on to law school but later moved into journalism. He was tall, athletic, and handsome—"the Hunk" in media circles—with the spark and wit of his father. Expectations of a political career had invariably fallen on Kennedy males, especially the first born, and he didn't rule out running for office. Jackie was fiercely proud of both her children.

In late 1993, Jackie discovered a lump and she was diagnosed as having developed non-Hodgkin's lymphoma. She began a grueling course of chemotherapy, but when the cancer spread inexorably she asked for treatment to be stopped. She took the news stoically, comforted by the fact that she had helped her children recover from their devastating early loss and guided them into adulthood. She died on May 19, 1994, in New York, at the age of 64, and was buried alongside Jack, Camelot's anointed leader and his elegant, cultured, effortlessly stylish consort reunited in death.

Five years later, tragedy struck the family once again. With his pinup-boy looks as well as hallowed last name, John F. Kennedy Jr. made headlines as he forged a legal career—

he was an assistant District Attorney in Manhattan—and when he launched the political magazine, *George*, in the mid-1990s. He dated a string of celebrity beauties before marrying Carolyn Bessette in 1996, but three years later both perished, along with Carolyn's sister Lauren, when an aircraft piloted by Kennedy Jr. crashed into the Atlantic off Martha's Vineyard. He was 38.

JFK Jr. was not the first of his generation to fall victim to the "Kennedy curse." Two of Robert Kennedy's sons had already died: David, from a drug overdose in 1984, a year short of his 30th birthday; and Michael, who was 39 when he was killed in a skiing accident in 1997. Ted's daughter Kara, who had a fatal heart attack in 2011, survived her father by only two years.

Ted himself had had a lucky escape in a plane crash in 1964, and five years later he was behind the wheel of the car that plunged off a bridge at Chappaquiddick Island and claimed the life of his passenger, Mary Jo Kopechne. The mystery surrounding the events of July 18, 1969, dogged Kennedy, who admitted leaving the scene of an accident that went unreported for several hours. Even after passing up the opportunity of bidding for presidency in 1972 and 1976, the incident was still at the forefront when he finally launched his campaign for the White House in 1980. He lost the Democratic nomination to incumbent Jimmy Carter, but served as Senator for Massachusetts from 1962 until his death in August 2009.

Eunice Kennedy Shriver died in the same month as her youngest brother. The first decade of the new century also witnessed the passing of Rosemary and Patricia, leaving Jean Kennedy Smith the sole survivor among JFK's siblings—the last of that first dynastic wave spawned from the union of Joseph P. Kennedy and Rose Fitzgerald almost one hundred years ago. The words of John Fitzgerald Kennedy, that "the torch has been passed to a new generation," are as apposite today with regard to this remarkable family—America's royalty—as they were in that galvanizing inaugural address of January 20, 1961, which made a nation believe anything and everything was possible.

Lightning strikes twice

Opposite above: May 14, 1965, Runnymede, England. Seven-year-old Caroline Kennedy is overwrought at a memorial service for her father. Queen Elizabeth II dedicated a stone monument at the place where the signing of Magna Carta took place in 1215, a landmark in British constitutional history.

Opposite below: Robert Kennedy on the campaign trail in Detroit in May 1968, his sights firmly set on that year's presidential election. After leaving Lyndon Johnson's government, he became a thorn in the White House incumbent's side as U.S. Senator, particularly over the Vietnam conflict. Kennedy's supporters urged him to declare his candidacy after the failure of the Tet Offensive early in 1968, when LBJ's fortunes were weak. He stayed his hand until Senator Eugene McCarthy's strong showing in the New Hampshire primary in March dealt a humiliating blow to Johnson.

Above: RFK basks in the afterglow of victory in the California primary, June 4, 1968. The Democratic nomination was not assured—Vice President Hubert Humphrey had entered the race, although too late to contest the primaries—but success in California was a major boost. Kennedy's victory address to his campaign team at the Ambassador Hotel, Los Angeles, was his last. He was shot minutes later, a crime for which disaffected Palestinian Sirhan Sirhan was convicted but which still attracts speculation of a wider conspiracy.

Jackie marries again

Left: October 20, 1968. Jackie marries Aristotle Onassis on his private island, Skorpios. Onassis had proposed the previous spring, when Bobby Kennedy was a front-runner in the presidential election. The Kennedys were unhappy about her choice of suitor and Jackie had agreed to defer the wedding until after the election. The marriage had already broken down by the time Onassis died in 1975.

Opposite: Jackie , John Jr., and Caroline pictured in Greece before the wedding.

Below: Family matriarch Rose Kennedy, pictured with her sole surviving son in 1970. Elected to the Senate in 1962, Teddy was widely expected to mount his own presidential campaign during the decade following the loss of his two brothers. He finally made his bid in 1980, only to find that the Chappaquiddick incident 11 years earlier still hung over him.

JFK Library is completed

Left: October 1, 1979, Boston, Massachusetts. Jackie and John Jr. at the dedication ceremony for the John Fitzgerald Kennedy Library. As this was a project that Jack himself had initiated, its completion had a special resonance for the family. Both Caroline and John Jr. spoke at the ceremony, the latter reciting Stephen Spender's poem "I Think Continually Of Those Who Were Truly Great." Jackie was fiercely proud of both her children as they entered adulthood. She was especially pleased at the way they were able to honor their father's name without allowing the past to overshadow their lives.

Below: June 5, 1980. Caroline is congratulated by members of her family after graduating from Radcliffe College, Harvard. Caroline's looks were more Kennedy than Bouvier, but she shared her mother's passion for horses and photography.

A new generation

Above: Caroline Kennedy, Arnold Schwarzenegger, Maria Shriver, and Tom Carney celebrate the June 1980 wedding of Bobby's daughter Courtney Kennedy and television executive Jeff Ruhe. Caroline parted from her writer boyfriend Carney soon after and met husband Edwin Schlossberg while working at the Metropolitan Museum of Art. They married in 1986, the same year that Schwarzenegger and Shriver tied the knot.

Left: John F. Kennedy Jr. and Carolyn Bessette Kennedy pictured in May 1999.

John Jr. graduated from Brown University in 1983 and after a working break went on to law school. After passing the bar exam, he served as a prosecutor in the Manhattan District Attorney's office, before moving into journalism.

Jackie died on May 19, 1994, so she did not live to see John Jr. marry Carolyn Bessette on September 12, 1996. There were rumors that John Jr. intended to move into politics himself, but on July 16, 1999, he, his wife Carolyn, and her sister Lauren were killed when the small plane John was piloting crashed into the sea off Martha's Vineyard, Massachusetts.

One of the greatest leaders of our time

Above: Arnold Schwarzenegger became a member of the extended Kennedy clan to run successfully for office when he was elected Governor of California in the recall election of 2003. Also pictured at the swearing-in ceremony are his then wife, Maria Shriver, and her parents, the late Sargent Shriver and Eunice Kennedy Shriver. The Republican "Governator" served two terms in office, stepping down in 2011. He and Shriver separated the same year, their 25-year marriage ending in the wake of news that Schwarzenegger had fathered a child by one of the household staff.

Left: August 12, 2009: Barack Obama presents the Presidential Medal of Freedom to the late Kara Kennedy, who received America's highest civilian award on her father, Edward Kennedy's, behalf. The honor was bestowed upon a man who "has served in the United States Senate for 46 years, and has been one of the greatest lawmakers—and leaders—of our time."

Passing the torch

Above: Presidential hopeful Barack Obama shared a joke with fellow Democrats Edward Kennedy and the latter's son Patrick at a rally in Washington, January 2008. Patrick Kennedy had become the youngest family member to hold office when he was elected to the Rhode Island House of Representatives in 1988, at age 21. However, in 2008 it was the Illinois Senator who was the recipient of Kennedy admiration and support. "I felt more and more certain that history had handed us that rarest of figures, one who could truly carve out new frontiers," said Ted in his effusive endorsement of Obama's candidacy. Caroline Kennedy concurred, saying that he had the inspirational qualities her father possessed. Edward Kennedy, the "Lion of the Senate" and tireless campaigner for health-care reform, died in August 2009, 19 months after Obama took office. Eunice Kennedy Shriver passed away that same month, leaving Jean Kennedy Smith the sole survivor among John F. Kennedy's eight siblings, and the torch firmly in the hands of a new generation.

Chronology

1914

October 7   Joseph P. Kennedy marries Rose Fitzgerald.

1915

July 25   Joe Jr. is born, eldest son of Joseph and Rose Kennedy.

1917

May 29   John Fitzgerald Kennedy is born, second son of Joseph and Rose. Within the next few years he is followed by four daughters: Rosemary, Kathleen "Kick," Eunice, and Patricia.

1925

November 20   Robert "Bobby" Francis Kennedy is born, third son of Joseph and Rose.

1928

February 20   Jean is born, youngest daughter of Joseph and Rose.

1929

July 28   Jacqueline Bouvier is born, elder daughter of Janet and John "Black Jack" Bouvier.

1932

February 22   Edward Moore Kennedy is born, fourth son of Joseph and Rose.

1936

JFK goes to Harvard to study political science.

1938

June   Joe Sr. goes to London with his family as U.S. ambassador to the Court of St. James.

1939

JFK takes a six-month sabbatical from Harvard to travel around Europe. His experiences lead to his first book, *Why England Slept*, which was based on his thesis and becomes a best seller. His travels also kindle JFK's ongoing interest in international affairs.

1940

JFK leaves Harvard with a bachelor's degree.

1943

March   After signing up for military service, JFK is made captain of PT-109, stationed in the Solomon Islands, South Pacific.

August 2   PT-109 is rammed by a Japanese destroyer in the Pacific Ocean and explodes. Two crew members are killed, but JFK ensures the survival of the remainder of the crew and was eventually awarded the Navy and Marine Corps Medal for his bravery.

1944

June   JFK enters hospital for back surgery.

August 12   Joe Jr. is killed on a bombing mission over France, and Joe Sr.'s political ambitions become focused on his second son.

1945

In London as a special correspondent for Hearst newspapers, JFK becomes violently ill—possibly with Addison's disease, a failure of the adrenal glands—and has to return to the United States.

1946

June   JFK is elected as the Democratic candidate in primaries for Massachusetts' 11th District.

November 5   After beating the Republican candidate, JFK is elected to Congress.

While in Europe on a fact-finding mission, JFK becomes ill again and Addison's disease is confirmed. He returns to the United States, so ill that last rites are administered, but later cortisone treatment keeps the condition in check.

1947

Jacqueline Bouvier enrolled at Vassar College, spending two years there before embarking on a year of study in France. On returning to the United States, she transferred to George Washington University in Washington, D.C., from where she graduated with a Bachelor of Arts degree in French literature.

1948

May 13   Kathleen "Kick" Kennedy is killed in a plane crash in France.

1951

June   Jackie Bouvier and JFK meet for the first time at a dinner party.

1952

Jackie is appointed "Inquiring Camera Girl" at the *Washington Times-Herald*.

1953

January   JFK takes his seat in the senate.

September 12   JFK marries Jacqueline Bouvier in Newport, Rhode Island.

1954

October   A risky double-fusion back operation leads to an infection and coma, and last rites are again administered to

JFK, but he pulls through. After a long convalescence, he finally returns to Capitol Hill in May 1955.

1956

January 1   JFK publishes *Profiles in Courage*, which documented figures in U.S. political history who had stood up for their principles. It becomes an instant best seller.

Democrat presidential candidate Adlai Stevenson throws open his choice of running mate to a vote, and JFK is beaten by Estes Kefauver. However, this proves a blessing in disguise when the subsequent election is a landslide for the Republicans.

August 23   A pregnant Jackie is rushed to hospital, but a baby girl is stillborn, JFK out of the country in the Mediterranean.

1957

November 27   Caroline Bouvier Kennedy is born, first child to JFK and Jackie. JFK becomes a doting father.

1958

JFK is up for reelection for Senator, but is returned to the Senate with a majority of 73.6 percent of the vote, the largest majority ever recorded in a Massachusetts election for Senator.

1960

January 2   JFK formally announces his candidacy for President of the United States, and enters several primaries to maximize his chances.

November 9   After a close result against Richard Nixon, JFK is confirmed as the President-elect and makes his acceptance speech at Hyannis Port.

November 23   John F. Kennedy Jr. is born, second child to JFK and Jackie.

1961

January 20   JFK is inaugurated as the 35th President of the United States.

January 30   First State of the Union address by JFK.

March 1   Founding of the Peace Corps.

April 17   A CIA-planned invasion of Cuba—which the new administration had inherited from the old—quickly turns into a disaster. It becomes known as the Bay of Pigs, after the landing site. Although JFK feels he was misled about the facts when he agreed to the operation going ahead, he accepts responsibility for the fiasco.

April   JFK meets the British Prime Minister Harold Macmillan in Washington, the start of a successful relationship between the two leaders.

May 5   The United States put their first man into space, one month after the Russians.

May   JFK and Jackie embark on an official European tour, in which JFK meets Charles

Above: The Kennedys on Inauguration Day.

de Gaulle in France, the Russian president Nikita Khrushchev in Vienna, and attends a banquet in London hosted by Queen Elizabeth II of Great Britain.

September 13   Signing of the Crime Bill, the start of a war in the United States against organized crime.

December 19   Joe Kennedy has a massive stroke and is no longer able to give his son advice and support.

1962

February 20   John Glenn becomes the first man to orbit the earth.

May 19   Marilyn Monroe sings "Happy Birthday" to the President at a gala evening to celebrate his forthcoming 45th birthday.

August Jackie takes Caroline to Italy for an extended vacation, bringing criticism from American citizens who felt she should be supporting her husband. She eventually returns home at the end of the month.

October 22 After Russia places nuclear warheads in Cuba, JFK announces a "quarantine line"—effectively a blockade. Two days later Russian ships approach the quarantine zone, but turn back. Eventually, a Soviet withdrawal is agreed in return for a promise that the United States will not invade Cuba.

November JFK signs the first of a series of Civil Rights legislation designed to end discrimination.

1963

June 11 After riots in Alabama, JFK announces that far-reaching civil rights legislation to end discrimination on the grounds of race, color, sex, or religion will be brought before Congress within days.

June 26 While addressing a huge crowd in West Berlin, JFK makes his famous "Ich bin ein Berliner" speech, which contrasts democracy and freedom with the repression of Communist regimes.

August 7 Patrick Bouvier Kennedy, third child of JFK and Jackie, is born five weeks' premature; he dies two days later from a respiratory problem.

October 7 The nuclear test-ban treaty is signed between the United States and Russia; although it excludes underground testing it is an important first step in halting the arms race.

November 1 After JFK gives the green light, a military coup in South Vietnam removes the anti-Communist government due to its persecution of the country's Buddhists. JFK later changes his mind about supporting the rebels after senior advisors voice serious objections, but it is too late.

November 22 During a trip to Dallas, JFK is shot twice and dies later that day. Within

hours, Vice President Lyndon Johnson is sworn in as the 36th President of the United States.

November 24 Lee Harvey Oswald, the suspect in custody for the shooting of JFK, is himself shot by Jack Ruby, a Dallas nightclub owner.

November 25 Funeral of JFK; he is buried at the National Cemetery in Arlington.

1964

September 24 The Warren Commission report concludes that Lee Harvey Oswald acted alone in the assassination of President Kennedy.

1968

June 5 Presidential candidate Bobby Kennedy is shot and dies the following day. Sirhan Sirhan is convicted and sentenced to death, subsequently commuted to life imprisonment.

October 20 Jackie marries Greek shipping tycoon Aristotle Onassis.

1969

July 18 Mary Jo Kopechne dies at Chappaquiddick, an incident that blights Edward Kennedy's presidential hopes.

November 18 Death of Joseph P. Kennedy.

1975

March 15 After the death of Onassis, Jackie returns to New York and begins work as a book editor, first with Viking and then with Doubleday.

1979

The House Select Committee on Assassinations concludes that JFK's death was the result of "probable conspiracy," overturning the lone-gunman conclusion of the Warren Commission.

1984

April 25 David Kennedy—the fourth of Bobby and Ethel Kennedy's 11 children—dies from a drug overdose.

1986

July 19 Caroline Kennedy marries Edwin Schlossberg.

1994

May 19 Jacqueline Kennedy Onassis dies and is buried alongside JFK at Arlington.

1995

January 22 Rose Kennedy dies, at the age of 104.

1996

September 12 John Kennedy Jr. marries Carolyn Bessette.

1997

December 31 Michael Kennedy—the sixth of Bobby and Ethel Kennedy's 11 children—dies in a skiing accident.

1999

July 16 John Jr., his wife Carolyn, and her sister Lauren are killed when the small plane he is flying crashes into the sea off Martha's Vineyard, Massachussetts.

2005

January 7 Death of Rosemary Kennedy, eldest daughter of Joseph and Rose Kennedy.

2006

September 17 Death of Patricia Kennedy Lawford.

2009

August 11 Death of Eunice Kennedy Shriver.

August 25 Death of Edward Kennedy, a year after being diagnosed with a malignant brain tumor.

2011

September 16 Kara Kennedy, daughter of Edward Kennedy and his first wife, Joan, has a fatal heart attack.